# THE SKIN BENEATH THE SHEETS

Written By, LoNette Grant

The Skin Beneath the Sheets is a work of fiction. The locations, names, incidents, and characters are used fictitiously. Any similarities between actual events, locations, or people, whether living or serendipitous.

ISBN 978-1-7347212-0-1
EBook ISBN 978-1-7347212-1-8

Cover photography by Veronica Wylie
Cover design by Veronica Wylie

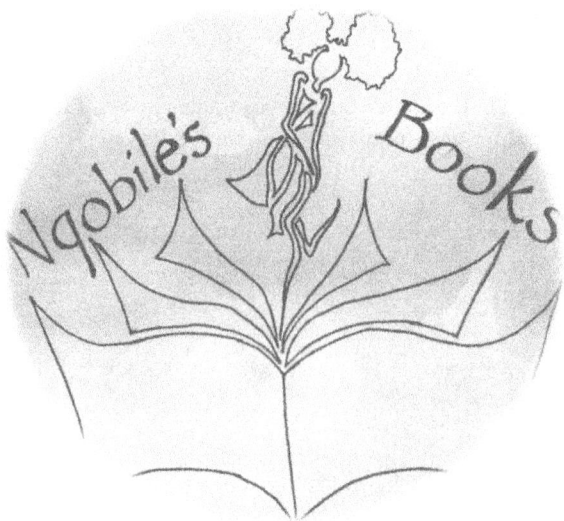
Nqobile's Books

Thank you to the many people who have assisted me in developing my identity as a black woman, as a writer, and as a dedicated believer in Christ. You all have assured me that whatever story I need to tell is a story that needs to be heard.

*To my father who lead me down intellectual pathways using books as stepping stones, and words as symbols that greater things were ahead. To my mother whose tears and tenacity taught me the unspoken lesson that merely good enough was never good enough.*
*I thank the both of you. Without your struggles, failures, successes, and histories; I might have never come to believe that I had something worthwhile to say, and that there might be ears prepared to hear it.*

There are SO many more of you who helped to form and inform me. Your presence in my life is priceless, and I am eternally grateful. Thank you.

# PROLOGUE

Peter drank almost a full 5th of whiskey on his own. With each glass he poured, he attempted to drown out the misery that threatened to overtake him. Sorrows and failures floated to memory… gulp. They were washed out to sea. Unrequited love attempted to shake up his calm demeanor, but another gulp stilled his ship. Disappointments he'd been cursed to receive and blessed to extend replaying non stop beneath his blinking eye lids only slowed when he took a swig from his glass, filled with liquid forgiveness. No, he could not ask forgiveness from those he was aware he had loved unsuccessfully. He mused inwardly about the possibility of apologizing, but could not bring himself to do either. His asking forgiveness… apologizing… Hell, allowing his mind to even think about what had transpired that night meant admitting his role in things. He wasn't guilty. He hadn't actually done anything himself. It was them… Sure he could have spoken up, but what exactly would that have accomplished?

He had to let those thoughts go, he had to shed this albatross that continually choked the length of his neck. Each day he breathed, he inhaled painful remembrance and exhaled sanity. As guilt crept in, his piece of mind escaped and he was left only with himself, the empty sound of rattling ice cubes, and clinking glass. Lost in his morose thoughts, the loud silence interrupted his sadness and he was brought back to reality by the sound of the ice chattering in his cup as he swayed it mindlessly in his raised hand.

No, no… he did not have the option of asking for forgiveness. Though he was guilt stricken, he rationalized that he had not actually committed the sin himself. His grandfather was guilty, and his father… his father was a dishonest disgrace to the cloth. But he, the man drowning himself in sips of sorrow saturated with silent contrition… he himself was guilty only of ignorance. The only thing he'd done was stumble upon his father's secrets. Why then was he riddled with such guilt? Why was he consumed when he knew there was nothing he could have done? There were questions that neither he nor his glass of Whiskey could answer. The warmth his throat felt as each sip poured into his body and set his soul ablaze with numbness was soothing. He was a man on fire. The heated sensation he felt did answer one question in particular though… What would bring him enough comfort to allow his eyes to close in slumber?

Inhaling deeply, he sucked in the last bits of pain enveloping his being. Slowly he exhaled his anxieties, willing them to stay away. He breathed again, one last time before gulping the remaining liquor from the glass and then from the bottle. With that, he sighed, crossed his arms and allowed his mind to drift lazily asleep. "Jesus," he mumbled. "Jesus," he breathed in His essence and expelled His name in the peace of sleep.

*  *  *

*I became my father*
*And I never even knew it*
*I became my father*
*And only Jesus helped me do it*
*  *  *

# CHAPTER 1

The screams were painful at least, and completely debilitating at best. Women I'd never seen wearing anything short of a maids uniform, and a potent smile to compliment closely ironed kinks bore only a nightgown and the despair of the death of their husbands. Children cried uncontrollably, knowing not only the fate of the men who desired freedom enough to die for it, but that they could do nothing but accept the charred love that once burned with the warming intensity of the sun. Could this really be the men they'd called father earlier that day? Neighbors comforted each other knowing things would never be the same, but would always be the same. The staleness of forced complacency filled the air, and it choked those present when they breathed it in.

They had taken the beatings like tough men. Refusing to breathe in the hate their attackers breathed out. Each blow landed with a grunt and eventually moans as they did what they'd vowed they would. Remained strong. But the beatings had not killed them, nor had the torturous hours that ensued. They answered no questions, replying to everything only. "There is no freedom without struggle," and "to live is Christ, but to die is gain." How odd was it that their freedom was not merely in their faith, it was also in the truth of the moment, and the promise of forever?

There was no end times fear in this town amongst them. Today was their end time, and we the anti-christ. And still they loved us despite the painful existence we'd given them...

They had burped me, held me when I cried, potty trained me, welcomed me home from school, taught me my manners and the true meaning of loyal friendship. They had done these things knowing full well that years later, their lessons would be forgotten and I would become a part of the movement that denied their humanness and threatened to choke out their love. But I would not win. I could not win because God's favor was on them. They existed in an emotional and physical turmoil which I could inflict and might never conceive of; but the fullness of their faith, rich like chocolate bars and flavored with sprinkles of bitterness and joy was even further from my understanding.

Certainly people should have noticed my pale skin as I cried for unknown reasons into a sea of brown. The beginning of my tears would be the end of their sorrow if I could help it. Had the lynching not have happened that night, I would have been the strangest sight on this side of the tracks. But on this night in particular my presence went unnoticed to most, and the rest... the rest chided me with eyes blazing with fear, confused contempt, and unconditional love. Though I tried to tell myself their anger was misplaced, something on the inside of me knew that their grief was real and one day would become real to me. They knew the secret to which I was not yet privy, but they loved me nonetheless.

At 8 years old, I had been asleep in bed when I heard car doors slamming. No lights, only deafening silence and the uninvited entry of squeaking metal into my dreams. Peering out of the window I saw cars screech away, but thought little of it. I got up to tell my parents what I'd seen, about the fat scary man from the store screaming, "hey boys! Let's put some niggers in their place tonight!" But as I knocked at my mother's door I heard muffled cries from the couch. "He's... He's asleep Peter, just like you need to be." I mused, "if he's asleep, why are you crying?" Only the singing of cicadas answered me. "Mommy, why do you cry when daddy is asleep? Are there monsters under your bed too?" With genuineness, I placed a small hand on her shoulder and the other on her knee. Her face remained buried between the valleys of her of her long soft fingers, so I squatted as best I could. Bracing myself against her, I leaned forward until my face was only centimeters from her own. She pulled a hand away to reveal bloodshot eyes still leaking tears I'd only cried when there was a booboo on my elbow. "Oh Peter. My monster is in the bed, not under it." Confused, I said "I can kick his butt. I'm a big boy now," and then stepped back to reveal the lanky eight year old muscles she always admired. She chuckled, sighed, and told me to go to bed.

I nodded my head, but my legs refused to acknowledge her authority. I remained still until she removed her other hand and placed her elbows on her thighs. Exhaling as if it was the last breath she would ever take, she allowed her hands to hang like tree limbs pretending that the wind could not sway them. I crawled onto her lap, aware that she wanted to be alone, but feeling how much she needed to be comforted. I placed my arms around her neck and buried my small head in her bosom. "Its gonna be okay, that mean monster won't hurt you. Daddy will get him, he always gets my monsters..." She placed her chin atop my head, but said nothing as she cradled me in her arms.

Looking back, she was probably thinking loudly, "Daddis is the monster." After a brief silence, she whispered, "back to bed Peter." I smiled, believed I'd mader her feel better. Hopping down,

I ran through the hallway and then remembered something. I raced back as quick as I could and said breathlessly, "Mommy I love you." Before she could reply I turned and ran back to bed where my two older brothers lay sound asleep.

In the great expanse of the Mississippi night I heard engines revving and drunken cheers. Then I recognized my grandfathers voice, "Lets ride out boys." With unexpected ferocity, bright head lights blinded me as they burned through the bedroom window. When the cars turned away, I noticed my grandpa Amnon in the drivers side of his pickup truck.

I lay still in the silence doing my best to lure the sand man near my pillow. But my eyes were as open as my ears, and I felt drawn to the noise outside, beyond the protective darkness of my bedroom. Though I knew I should have stayed in my bed, my curiosity got the best of me and I eased the window open, careful that the wood did not creek loud enough to wake anyone. Pulling on my favorite tennis shoes, I slid my thin frame out of the window as I had always done, but was never supposed to do. The warmth of the June air protected my thin skin and I followed the cheers coming from the herd of cars traveling up County road 215.

When the cars finally stopped, I could hear young screams and hateful laughter. By the time I was close enough to see what was going on, the sounds of clubs and bats meeting flesh had ceased, but the death filled moans of two black men being tortured mercilessly invaded my ear drums. Peering through the hedges before me I saw seven hooded men, and a few with simple sheets adorned with eyes cut out like the masks I made at school.

The intrusive lights from their cars made it difficult to get a good look, so I crept closer and squatted beneath the brush so I wouldn't be seen. It was only then that I saw the bloody bodies of two men I knew quite well. Mr. Brown and Mr. Lee who frequented the laundromat my family owned. Mr. Brown's wife was a nurse at the Black clinic, and Mr. Lee's wife was my nanny and our maid. Panic overcame me and I searched for a familiar face among the brown ones peering from windows and crying on porches. But it seemed I knew no one. An entire world less than two miles away, and all I knew of it was blood pooling under the bruised bodies of the men who'd been nothing but nice to me. Why was all of this happening?

Crying frantically, I leaned forward and fell out of the bushes that had kept me hidden. Mrs. Lee saw me and yelled stop, but her cries only fed the fury of the sheeted men. Exposed now, and afraid that the men might get me too, I ran to her and wrapped my arms around her legs. Overwhelmed by terror, I buried my face in her skirt, barely noticing the six year old fingertips that reached for the same protection. It was Ruthy. I grasped her hand and stood holding her as she sobbed confusedly. The men grabbed Mr. Brown and Mr. Lee, jolting them to half lived attention. Another grabbed two nooses from the bed of a truck I would never forget, while the other retrieved a can of gasoline.

I shut my eyes just in time to miss the quick preparation, and prayed that it be over. I opened my eyes at the exact moment that both bodies were given permission to dangle. No sooner had the bodies slowed their twitching than the man doused them with gasoline making sure to empty it until the last drop. He walked away closing the bed of the truck and clapped his hands with excitement. A second hooded man rose from the truck that I thought belonged to my grandfather, and took a deep drag from his cigarette. He looked to a third and said, "they already dead, let's just go." But the other shook his head and said, "this is how it's supposed to be. Now you either do your part or you can join em' on that tree. Want some company fellas?!?" The first man sighed, took one last puff and bellowed, "The South shall rise again." With that he tossed his cigarette on the ground just beneath their bodies and laughed as the flames rose. When they were sure the bodies could not be saved, they piled in their pick-ups and left. The laughs were eerily familiar, but the hoods kept their identities secret.

The skin beneath the sheets would remain concealed by the lie of 50 count, stark white cowardice. Fear, anger, and confusion resided within me, and the only thing left to do was cry… Cry as Ruthy watched her father go down in flames. Was there anything to do beyond join in the shedding of tears and the pain of brown grief?

*\* \* \**

*His father gave him the gift of brokenness*
*And he blessed me with fragments of my own*
*\* \* \**

# CHAPTER 2

"**P**eter's not in right now, can I take a message?" I sat across the room motioning wildly to Ruthy, my wife of 35years. She smiled at me as she spoke to my sister Jane. When I heard her say I was gone, I sighed a deep sigh and gave her an energetic thumbs up to which she rolled her eyes. For a moment I thought perhaps she was angry with me. Feeling guilty I walked over to her thinking that flirting would fix her frustration. She pushed my hands away and steady streams of, "okay… okay, I'll let him know," poured from her lips. It was apparent that Jane was being particularly civil to her which was unbelievably strange.

At one time, Jane had been close to Ruthy, but when she discovered that I was in love with Ruthy things changed suddenly. Late night girl chats became tense moments and rolled eyes. Discussions about neighborhood boys, turned into awkward omissions of the hearts desires.

I felt guilty at times for ruining a promising friendship, but Ruthy never let me carry this guilt for long. The truth was, their friendship was superficial even at its most sincere moments. Their acquaintance only came about because Ruthy was forced at times to help her mother, my nanny. For all intents and purposes, Ruthy's mother had raised me. She bathed and burped me, cooked and cleaned the house, and saw me off to school. My mother, as loving as she was, was like a second mother to me, Ruthy like a sister. Jane, a year older than Ruthy, at first loved having Ruthy around. Ruthy was available at her every beck and call, even if it meant suppressing her own happiness to appease Jane.

Ruthy never liked this, and considered herself a slave to Jane's needs. It wasn't until Jane became aware of the intense love we felt for each other that she dismissed Ruthy and freed her of the friendship her brown skin had forced her to maintain. Jane had hated her ever since, so even the quietest of hello's sent Ruthy's way usually came with motives independent of sisterly adoration. The two of us had been in love since the night that neither of us desired to remember, but could never seem to forget. And though it had cost us both dearly, it was a love that neither of us was willing to relinquish.

"Pete... Pete, are you listening to me?" The choler of Ruthy's voice brought me back to the present moment. "I'm sorry babe, what were you saying?"
"That whole zone out thing used to be kind of sexy when we were growing up, but now it pops up at the most inopportune times... Focus," she chuckled gingerly then sucked her teeth. Smiling tightly, she continued. "Why don't you sit down, I have to tell you something."

"Tell me what? My sister called... She only calls when she wants something, so what did she want this time? Money... Does she want me to beat up that psychotic boyfriend of hers?! Go ahead." Reclining back in my favorite chair I said, "lay it on me. I'm ready for it." Ruthy looked at me with disdain. No matter how she had felt about Jane in the past, she refused to fester with anger. Jane was my sister and Ruth believed whole heartedly that she and I ought to mend things between us, and that I should support her no matter what. "I don't know what you're waiting for, I'm sitting." I chuckled as I mused about which creative scenario Jane had concocted this time to get more of my attention. "Ruthy, lay it on me already... I've gotta go get the kids from school in a minute and I don't really have time to play an hour long guessing game. Just tell me what she wants so I can decide how quickly I ought to say no." Ruthy sighed heavily, slapping her own forehead in exasperation. "This is important Peter." I could tell that my candor was irritating, she only called me Peter when she was irritated with me. "Okay, Ruthy poot," when I said this she rolled her eyes playfully, "look I'm sorry... I'm ready, I really am." I threw my hands up in surrender, but my attitude remained stained with splotches of smug sarcasm. "Peter John Thomas! This is serious. Jane was calling about your father!"

I cocked my head to the side confused about why she would bring him up. I had not seen my father in years, and she knew why. Over the years I'd barely even accepted his phone calls. "What about him?" My tone was dry, but curious. She sternly stared me in the face and without blinking an eyelid said, "He is dying." My breath escaped me, as did whatever words I might have uttered if I could comprehend the passing moments. "I wasn't ready." Was there a word that could describe the multitude of emotions flowing through my mind? Absolutely not. The only thing I seemed to be able to able to muster was the impassioned blinking of my eyelids, and a mouth gaping open, from which warm air escaped blocking the formation of words and thoughts.

After a pregnant silence, during which Ruthy gazed warmly into my eyes which had pooled with warm tears, my words flew out before I could stop them. "I'll be back. I have got to get the kids."

Her jaw dropped, and for the first time she looked as shocked as I felt. I stood, picking imaginary lint from my dress pants and clergy collar. Walking toward the door, I paused a full second. "Will you pack my bags?" I yawned and then rubbed my eyes, hoping to fool her into believing that I was not troubled. "By the time you get back I will have all of our bags packed." She smiled painfully, silently pledging to support me. I cloaked my broken spirit in blunt arrogance, but she always saw through me. "You will not be alone in this. We will go with you. I will call Deacon Mark, and he can take your place at the church until we get back. It will be fine, and until it gets fine, I will be by your side." My eyes said I love you, but my lips said nothing. I kissed her, and walked away before her kisses caused my wall to breakdown, and I fell apart.

*\* \* \**

*He handed me the imperfections of humanness*
*And I developed flaws to be shown*
*\* \* \**

# CHAPTER 3

It would have been nice to have rain that morning. Even a fresh blanket of morning dew might have squelched the flames of frustration which would be fanned late that night. In retrospect, anything would have been better for me... Better for us and everyone else involved for that matter. My eyes discovered late night truths that stole aspects of my innocence... my faith. Silence, and screams both proved to be painfully loud in the ears of a 6 year old girl. My eardrums sopped up the ruckus that fought mercilessly to break them down. There would be forever moments that followed. Moments during which the sounds of that fatal night played and replayed until crackling fire consumed my eardrums. Volumes never altered, only stretches of time that paralyzed my body. Images that had burned into my retinas would reappear at the most uncomfortable times. Crowds of people were forever filled with the men who'd stolen our freedom that night.

There were no words to express the amount of fear I felt the night of my fathers death. Between my mothers screams and the devilish eyes of the hooded white men who stood on the clay of the earth entertained by the pain of execution, I realized that night at the age of 6, that there was no time to consider the end times. That night was my end; the end of the world as I knew it.

Did I understand the difference between life and death? No, but I understood the smell of burning flesh, and experienced the fear that only the shameless screams of a man on fire can elicit. As blood oozed from his wounds, happiness oozed from my soul. Blood laced the dust that had once covered my feet while I sang, "Little Sally walker, sitting in her saucer…" and danced with other girls until my mother called me in. Where would I dance now? Could I ever sing with joy, knowing that the very dust on which I stood had soaked up the remnants of my fathers humanity?

He had been so perfect, and suddenly he was in perfect pain… Not the perfect peace he had preached about. Where had our perfect peace gone!? It had disappeared with my mother's dignity. Had she ever cried like this before? Begged with the fervor of a child trying to get a cookie instead of the whoopin' her parents felt she deserved. At 6, I struggled to recall having ever seen her cry at all. Every time she wailed I tensed more and there was nothing I could do to save either of them. My mother's hope died with my father, and the young faith I had, left from my frame seemingly giving life to the flame that licked his toffee skin. Jesus died hanging from a tree, and my father hung from a tree… And so did my uncle Manasseh Brown. But they were not Jesus.

I swam in thoughts too unfathomable for my mind to grasp. It was like diving into the deep end of the pool with no lesson or life jacket. My screams and cries though loud and haunting even for me could not be heard over any of the others. What had my mother and I done to warrant the nauseating sights from that night? Those questions had no answer, so I shut down. My tears continued, but my cavernous mouth closed. My balled fists clung to my mothers dress, and I turned down the communal volume. The silence was eerie, but eerie was far better than what remained playing in my mind.

Oh God how I wished for the rain that never came.

Suddenly a small frame as white as the skin beneath the sheets of the hooded men ran toward me. I hid my face in my mother's housecoat hoping that my eyes deceived me and my life would be spared. I felt a small hand grasp mine and peered down to see shoed feet staring up at me. Glancing around my mother's legs, I realized that a white boy wearing only his shorts and shoes clenched my mothers skirt as tightly as I. He must have noticed me too, because he stepped behind my mother quickly and held me in his arms. I held him too. I would carry the pains of this night with me forever, along with the momentary comfort of my friend Peter. My mother brushed each of our shoulders lightly. She could not console us because her own grief was so great, but she tried.

I never questioned Peter's presence, I just knew that God was in the moment. Peter was my comforter. Would another man ever hold me like my father always had? That moment with Peter, though short lived, was all the comfort I could take. No questions, no words, no outward expressions. We both understood that the other was hurt, and remained hurt together until the men felt comfortable enough to retreat from the chaos they had created.

How long we were there, I never knew. Watches were not a luxury we could afford. But God cried with Peter and I. He held us together, and he gave us everything that his word promised in that bitter hour. In those moments we had found that which we did not yet understand. That which others spent a lifetime in search of… eternal love, and the enticing struggle for truth and freedom.

\* \* \*

*I swallowed his despair*
*Chewed on his anger*
*And inhaled his confusion*
\* \* \*

# CHAPTER 4

There isn't a day that goes by that I don't think about my father. Everything I remember about him exuded grace, wisdom, and strength. All these years later, it STILL blew my mind that a man could be so Godly and yet be so hated by those claiming to love the very same God. When did it become so wrong to want your humanness acknowledged? Was his entire crime telling a man that his name wasn't boy?

Everyday that I was blessed to see him, I wanted to be a man just like him. His life didn't matter to the men behind the masks, but it mattered to me. He died with Godly pride in his eyes. He died knowing that his work had been completed and that I understood what it really meant to live. They thought that his pride died with him. They thought that making me look him in his eyes while he died would strike a chord of fear somewhere in me. But it didn't; that pain in his eyes struck an entirely different chord. I told myself that the smirk gracing his lips after his last twitches ceased wasn't pain. Instead it was a show of his victory. Not only had he died in the manner in which he lived, but he had instilled a fearless resolve within me. I would not live caged by my fear, nor trapped by their assumptions about me. I would live and die with dignity.

The recollection I had of my fathers murder wasn't quite as poetic for me as it had been for Ruthy. Fear, anger, and helplessness took turns waving at my eyes as they fired off through my synapses.

We were just getting to bed that night. The day had been hot, sticky, and beyond busy. My mother was excited that day because our neighbor had killed a few hogs, and was kind enough to share some pork chops with us. That's how it was back then. If one person in the neighborhood ate, we all ate. It didn't matter whether the only thing you had to offer your neighbor was a cucumber, or pot liquor from the days greens. No one went to bed completely hungry. Whatever we had to spare, we shared. Whatever they had to spare they shared. Though it was no surprise for any of us to look out for each other, it was always a welcomed reminder that God saw our pain and would make provision for us as we did His work. Mamma welcomed the pork chops excitedly and fried them along with some green tomatoes, rice, and squash she had pulled from the small garden outside. As always, she had taken something simple and fastened together a full meal. We were never allowed to eat until Daddy came home and had gotten the first piece.

We ran with extra excitement that day. Bouncing up and down through the tall brush, wrestling, and laughing like we had not a care in the world. I guess in retrospect, I should have known better. Should've known that the peace I felt was not peace at all. It was the ignorance of my youth intermingled with the thickness of the moist Mississippi heat. It was the ironic poetry of getting medicinal red clay caked onto my good pair of pants and hoping that I didn't get a painful whoopin' because of it; while I had heard my father speak candidly of the African blood that stained the clay and was spilled simply because it could be spilled. Here I was enjoying trees my forefathers had hung from and finding a particularly comforting shield from the sun beneath the very tree my father would hang from. Was it ironic or twisted that against my mothers wishes, I had climbed that very same tree, found the strongest branch, and fallen asleep listening to the symphony of cicadas, chirping birds, and still air? It was only when I had grown a little too comfortable in that tree and perhaps rested too long that I fell from the tree and graced the moss patched clay with a square thud. The same thud I heard when we cut my father down.

The emotions I felt at being held by men who ordinarily would have done anything in their power to avoid touching me sent indescribable shockwaves through my body. Between the burning rage I felt from their hands on my poorly clad shoulders, and the burning my eyes experienced being held open, I could barely control myself. I saw every hit, every kick, and every cut. I watched helplessly as they screamed obscenities at my father, strung him up, and lit his body on fire. I watched as my mother and aunt cried useless tears knowing that no matter how loud they screamed or how much they begged, the abuse would not stop.

I saw Peter tumble through the bushes and I saw the electricity between he and Ruthy as they clung to my aunt and tried to console each other. I saw the anguish on neighbors faces, and felt the fear sweating from their pores. Who would insist that they vote now? Who would stand tall when danger was present and protect our communities most prized commodities; women and children? I saw some boys cower with fear hoping they wouldn't be next, and I saw others courageously protecting whoever they could. We saw each other. I knew in an instant that my father and my uncle had inspired more than me, but that I had to do something with my internal inferno.

I watched everything unwillingly, but I determined myself that I would never see another injustice for the rest of my life and simply watch it happen. My father had died the way he lived. My uncle stood strong until he could stand no longer. Their legacy was more than a lynching. It was the unwavering silent commitment I made that night to never run away from the fire, but to face it like a man.

*  *  *

*I grasped for fresh air*
*Clawed for sanity*
*And lifted my voice in confession*
*  *  *

# CHAPTER 5

My father and I had been estranged for sometime, and while I knew we would eventually reconnect, I had not expected this. Yet here I am, at my father's bedside hoping for one more chance to tell him that I love him. Of all of his children, my father and I were by far the closest, but life had pulled us in different directions. Sitting here at his bedside it all seemed unimportant now. An argument… Mean words… Rolled eyes… And lips curled so tight they'd abandoned the pink color of my flesh for the bland white of classroom chalk. I strained to remember but I drew only blanks. This angered me even more because I was staring at the man with whom I shared my DNA and the secrets of my childhood. Honestly, I can't even say what it was that we had argued about last. Whatever it was must have been big because I'd left Shubuta in 1971 and never looked back

I was staring at his closed blue eyes, the very eyes that had welcomed me into the tranquil depths that warmed his lids. I had prayed for eyes as blue as his, but my own brown irises held a simplicity that constantly kept me grounded. My nose held the shape of his. The length of our nasal bridges mirrored each other, though his held a slight curve that appeared shortly after my 8th birthday, making its home just below his eyes. My nose appeared wider only because of the weight I'd gained as an adult, which expanded my cheeks, lips, and nose. For all intents and purposes I was not merely my fathers keeper, I was his twin. We were alike. Though I'd still misplaced memories of the event that pushed me to run away with such anxiety, I only managed to recall exactly how badly I'd wanted to be like my father.

I touched his hands. Hands that had built our home from the ground up. Hands that used an ax to cut down trees, and slice through wood for fire. Those same hands put band-aids on my knees when I'd climbed a tree that I wasn't supposed to climb, and had collected both me and my pride from the ground when I tried to ride my bike for the first time without training wheels.

Yes, I'd desired my fathers hands, I'd even prayed that mine would grow to have the same size, strength, and power to touch lives that my fathers hands held. Today, my fingers which now shared the same nail beds as his, trembled with nervousness. Trying to steady myself, I traced along the lines of veins that appeared like green ropes beneath his skin. My hands had grown to be even larger than his, and had built even more than he had. God had blessed these hands of mine.

Would my veins announce my age like his? The veins on my grandfathers hands had mirrored tree rings. Each ring choking out whatever goodness he had left inside of him. I prayed that my veins would stop as the greenish tic-tac-toe lines that painted my fathers hands had, and would never reach the point of green snakes that had littered my grandfathers.

The white bed sheets he laid under had hidden his skin which now cowered beneath. I pulled the sheets back only to reveal his legs, void of the muscle that had once pumped energy into every one of his motions. Legs that had carried me to the hospital when I broke my own, and fought their way through the front door when my mother screamed for help because she couldn't escape

escape the smoke filling her lungs. My father was not the same man I had known. I had run away from a man who stood for what he believed in and masterfully displayed his strengths. My father had been my hero until the day he discovered I had chosen to attend bible college instead of medical school. I had only wanted to be like him, how could he not have understood that? Suddenly memories of the emotional day when I left my home came back like a flood.

The sun was bright that day, and its rays gave me every ounce of energy I'd needed. I was 19 years old and terrified to become the man I'd always said I wanted to become. I prepared myself for my father's anger, took one last deep breath and walked in the front door with my pregnant girlfriend Ruthy

My father's eyes bulged before I said anything. I held her hand tightly and told my parents that we needed to talk. We all sat in silence a moment. "I have some news," I began, "first, I will not be finishing my degree dad." I looked away when I saw his face growing slightly red, though the tip of his nose remained the color of peach, crayon box flesh. He cleared his throat, and I motioned for him to allow me to finish. "I will be attending Garrett-Evangelical Theological Seminary. We," I motioned to my Ruthy, "will be leaving… together… at the end of the summer." My mothers eyes pooled with tears, but she said nothing. "What happened to Rebecca? I thought you two were getting married." His eyes shifted smugly to Ruthy when he continued, "That's what you said… yesterday." Ruthy dropped my hand and her eyes darted to the window abandoning my manhood. I reached out to her but she held up her hand and leaned away refusing to let me see her cry. He smirked, certain that he was going to tear our relationship to shreds.

"You said you wanted me to marry her, I said I wasn't sure I loved her. In truth, I dated Becca to make you happy, but Ruthy and I are in love." She looked back at me, and then nervously smiled at the hardwood floor that protected her feet from the ground below. He pointed at Ruthy angrily and retorted, "You will not marry this girl."

"Why not!? She's a good girl, and we love each other." I couldn't understand his anger. Ruthy's mom had been my nanny, and we had always been close. He'd never complained about our relationship until that day. He continued, apparently vexed by the things I was telling him. "You will not marry her if you are to be a member of this family."

I nodded my head at first, then he said, "And there is no bible college. I raised a doctor, that's all there is to it." I simply replied, okay. "Ruthy, you need to leave, and you are no longer welcome here. Whatever you two have going on stops today. It's one thing to have a good time with one of them son, but today you have crossed the line!" My head had been lowered for so long, I never saw her lips part when she whispered, "But I'm pregnant Mr. Thomas, sir... I'm pregnant."

As I raised my eyes to look at my father, I felt his burning through me. I turned instead to look at the mother of my child who now gripped her small belly, easily swallowed up by her yellow sundress. Just as my eyes met hers, my fathers pale white hands met the cocoa of her right cheek. "Are you sassing me gal?! I said leave! And you better do it fast before I cut that little monkey out of ya!" I scrambled over to help her from the ground. When I was sure she was alright, I wrapped my arm around her and furiously told my father that I loved her and my mind was made up. He shouted angrily, using words my ears had never been exposed to at home. We turned to walk away and then he broke my heart, "If you walk out of that door, don't ever darken that frame again." We continued to walk out, and upon reaching the doorstep I lifted my chin, firmed my grip on Ruthy and whispered to no one in particular, "I'm sorry. Goodbye." My words of course were inconsequential, and the only one who accepted my apology was the warm breeze sweeping down Barner road.

Neighbors stared in amazement and horror as I cranked up my 65' chevy caprice and drove away. The moment I met with Count/z;y Road 215, I sighed, told Ruthy I loved her and drove until my eyes couldn't hold back the tears any longer and they blurred the road ahead. Somewhere in those tears was the wish I'd made to have my fathers hands.

Staring at my fathers hands kept my attention so long that I never noticed his eyes wildly fluttering. It wasn't until I felt them open and staring intently, gushing through the dams of my temples that I looked him square on. Our eyes locked, and I saw him breathe his last breath. Felt the wind escape from his body. My father would never know my innermost feelings. Maybe he didn't need to know that I had forgiven him, or maybe my eyes told it all. I prayed that my own brown eyes had confessed my hurt, my pain, my forgiveness… My God, I had just lost my father. If he were still alive, he might be able to offer a more… a more satisfactory reason for our distance than the one I have, but I doubt it. Without effort, I lowered my head and refused to weep. I already missed the skin which cowered beneath his stark white sheets.

\* \* \*

*I became my father*
*And I didn't want to*
\* \* \*

# CHAPTER 6

Time, like watches, was a luxury simply not afforded to most blacks in Mississippi. In times of grief, there was only time to mumble "yassuh" beneath our breath. No time for tears, fears, or pain. Only time to work at the behest of the people we knew hated us, and to hold it all together when our worlds fell apart. There was no time to hate them back, and there was no time to mourn the loss of our beloved men.

It wasn't until the following morning that I saw my cousin Ezekiel whose father had been all but crucified alongside my own. Zeke was a year older than me, and he appeared to have shed as many tears as I had. The moment I saw him, I sprang from the breakfast table and held on to him for dear life. We huddled together crying tears we'd kept in for far too long, knowing that our fathers were gone, but not fully understanding the weight we would be carrying for the rest of our lives.

"Children, we need to talk." Suddenly, it felt as if rocks and butterflies filled the stretch of my stomach. There was no time to wonder, and no space for assumptions. Our mothers would be leaving for work soon, and their eyes read all of the shattered hurries their lips could not quite utter. We walked to the table expeditiously. Zeke's mother began, "you both know what happened last night."

We nodded in nervous unison, expecting the worst news but hoping for the best. "Well, now that your fathers are gone, things are going to be tough." I burned with fury, wondering how things could possibly be tougher than they had been last night. Despite our feelings however, we were wise enough to know that talking back was simply not an option. We listened intently for the punch line. My mother could read my emotions. She started, "Money is going to be tight around here, tighter than it was before. So… Zeke and Aunty Martha are going to come live with us. How do you two feel about that?" She smiled, as she searched for confirmation from us. Ezekiel and I were elated to be living together, he had always been my best friend anyway. Zeke's smile widened, and then dropped suddenly. His head followed the curve of his lips. "But mommy, what happens to our things. Why can't we have our own house?"

Looking like her world had just collapsed, Aunty Martha drew him in and held him close, then sat back to look into his eyes. She answered as best she could, "Well. Uncle David… He owned this land. His daddy left it to him, but your daddy didn't own our house. The white men who-" she choked on her words trying to withhold tears which streamed hesitantly from invisible cracks in her eyes. My mother tried to interject, but Aunty Martha held up her hand. "The white men owned it, and now that daddy is gone they want it back." She said the last syllable with such righteous indignation that I thought angry fire might follow.

Zeke and I both understood that our lives would forever be stained by the blood and fire of the previous night. "I hate them! I hate all of them!" Zeke voiced the pain that my heart had been burying. "Next time they come through here, they betta' be ready, cuz' I'ma get em' all!"

He stood and marched toward the door as if he had a weapon large enough to overthrow the hate that littered their stark white bed sheets.

"I'm gonna tell you this one time and one time only Zeke. So you better hear… me… good." Zeke's steps slowed and he spun on his heels ferociously. He retorted in defiance, "Tell me what?!" Appalled at his aggression, Aunty Martha began to cry. As she pulled herself together, my mother hopped from her seat and snatched him at the pit of his arm. Though he attempted to wiggle himself free of her hold, the pained expression on his face said everything that we needed to know. Her lengthy middle and pointer fingers dug into the flesh that covered the meeting place of his bones. The fight between her grasp and his arm pit was a beastly one, but she'd won the moment she reached out. Her lips curled tightly until they nearly disappeared, "Sit down here. Try that again and I'll slap the black off ya!" Zeke eased into the seat and then shrunk away when her words maneuvered through his thoughts. She picked up where Aunty Martha had left off, this time addressing the both of us.

"Hate breeds more hate, it doesn't make it go away. Now, you can be mad, sad, or afraid… But hateful you will not be! Your daddies both died with godly pride, and starting today…we are walking in pride." She came close to Zeke's face and pointed a finger, "I don't have time for hate, and neither do you. That is foolishness! So you better get your little self together young man. Fix your face and live a life that would've made your daddy proud.

He did not die in vein! He did not! We are black… And white folk don't like that. But we all the same… we all bleed the same, we all breathe the same, and God love us all the same. You're daddy loved you. And he loved those cowardly white men even though they hated him. You said you wanted to be like yo' daddy… so this is a fine time to start! We don't hate, we love. That's what WE do. When you hate, you be just like them; causing more hate. You understand me boi?!" Zeke nodded, and she kissed his forehead gingerly. "Lord cover him… Keep us, give us strength. Ain't no time for weakness." She whispered to no one in particular, and I hoped that God heard her that morning.

Whispering to Zeke, though we all heard it she rocked gently and said, "In this house, we ain't got no time fa' hate. The best thing about us black folk is that God blessed us with the gifts of forgiveness and love. We love a world who don't love us… The best way to fix them… The best way to get em' back, is to live in a way where all they can do is love you . Don't be like them baby… All you got time to do is be better than them."

*  *  *

*I became my father*
*And I'm still me too*
*  *  *

# CHAPTER 7

These people didn't know my father. They were smiling, laughing, crying, and remembering his legacy. Was I the only person here feeling sickeningly uncomfortable? Even Ruthy and Zeke, it seemed had some fond memories of him. I on the other hand had memories of him that might have been fond had it not have been for the sheets that had enveloped his skin. He had been a masked coward… The devil between the sheets on my mother's bed. There had to be an explanation, but the only conclusion my mind could reach was that my father was a member of the most racist organization in America. He was a terrorist. He'd left a legacy in the town of Shubuta. They all knew him as an inspiring man, who had worked his way from nothing to great prosperity. He took the gospel to the streets, and carried God in the pocket of his very being. How then could the selfless person that we all knew and loved, carry such a hateful secret? One that even I hadn't discovered until this morning.

Though I had been angry with my father for years, I woke up this morning with forgiveness in my heart. I stared into the bathroom mirror, and saw only my fathers face searching my eyes for glimpses of love that I had hidden beneath my hurt. Smiling at the handsome mix of us both, I thought it only fitting that I wear one of his old necktie's.

There was a tie that I'd bought him years ago, he'd said it was his favorite. I decided that in the spirit of forgiveness, I ought to adorn myself with something that brought him pleasure. This would be the first moment that thoughts of his pleasure did not cause my own pain.

Strolling to my parents bedroom I could feel the cracking of the hardwood floor, and I glanced at the couch where my mother sat when she told me that the devil was in her bed. Feeling a sudden chill creep down my spine I took a deep breath and made my way to their old closet. His clothes had always hung on the right side. It had the least amount of space, but between the two of them he had the least amount of clothes. A simple man like him, needed only a few pairs of pants, a couple of shirts, and several tie's. Pulling the door further back, I discovered the necktie's he'd hidden from us, so we wouldn't put them on our heads and pretend to be a swamp thing. My eyes invaded his privacy, scanning each tie until my gaze fell upon his favorite.

I'd bought him the tie at 18. Silver and silk, it was the perfect width and length. A cross the color of water embellished the plain silk fabric. Partial scripture written in scarlet and burnt orange garnished the cross. "John 3:16 For God so loved the world; Romans 5:1 Therefore, since we have been justified through faith, we have peace with God; Philippians 4:13 I can do all things through Christ; Matthew 5:3 Blessed are the poor in spirit; Galatians 3:28 There is neither Jew nor Gentile, neither slave nor free, nor is there male and female, for you are all one in Christ Jesus." I didn't understand it at the time. Couldn't fathom why my fathers eyes welled up with tears the moment he saw it, then when he got to the last scripture, Galatians 3:28, he balled like a baby. I'd never seen him so contrite.

I tied his tie around my own neck, wiped my sentimental tears away, and fastened the matching cufflinks, which bore the initials P.T. Initials that we shared. My tear stained eyes abruptly fell upon my mother's old yellow dress. She reminded me of a sunflower, and every time I saw her in it, yellow became my favorite color all over again. As I pulled it from the closet, I saw garment bags tucked neatly away at the top. Ignoring them, I tugged at her dress and the bags tumbled from their place on the closet shelf. Curious, I pulled them out and laid them across my father's bed, slowly unzipping them one at a time.

White was all I saw at first. Confused, I pulled the zipper down the remaining way, and then fumed at my discovery. In the garment bag were two Klan robes, freshly pressed and still smelling of laundry detergent. Immediately, my mind began searching for a rational explanation. I checked the robe and saw the initials P.T. written inside of the sleeve, and along the neckline. My father wrote his initials in all of his clothing, and no one would have been in his closet to label his clothes unless he'd requested it. Were my eyes deceiving me, or had I just discovered the unthinkable? Was my father really the hooded monster in my mothers bed? Had white sheets really masked the hatred he breathed? Everything I had ever understood about my father was untrue, and my world was quickly unraveling. Having lost my breath, I struggled to breathe in the last bit of clarity and sanity available to me, but my body fought it. Gasping for air, I leaned my arms on the bed trying to still my legs, lungs,  and thoughts. Inhale… Exhale… I talked to myself, "think Pete think! What the hell is this?!" I paced uncontrollably, throwing back one reason after another, but knowing that every excuse was merely an excuse. There was no truth in fear filled bitter excuses.

"Peter are you ready?" I panicked when I heard the sound of Ruthy's voice nearing the doorway. "Uhhhh, just a minute." I zipped away my feelings and the white sheets that had once cloaked the man I'd loved, just in time to see Ruthy's beautiful cocoa skin appear in the doorway. I didn't even try to hide my confusion. Ruthy could read me like a book, I just hoped that she'd tune in to the explicit writing on the pages of my face and ignore the meaning behind my silent words. She searched my face for truth in my grief, but my eyes lied. They screamed fervently that my father's death had caused the fury of tears fighting to drop. If she listened closely, she might have heard the whispers from my soul, crying out for an explanation that no one could supply. Or maybe she had heard. Maybe in the silence between us, my whispers were loud enough to reach the drums tucked deep within her ears. Maybe, just maybe that was why her eyes fell upon the garment bag my fingers still gripped, though she never voiced the questions drowning her pupils. "Hey tough guy, I'm ready when you are," she sang as she turned and left the room. Tough guy... That had always been her way of telling me 'you can do this.' "Ruthy, can I ask you something?"

Without slowing her steps she shrugged, "of course honey. My ear is all yours." I was silent a moment, and she called to our youngest grandchildren that it was time to leave for the funeral. I placed my pale hand on her shoulder, and the stark contrast between her skin and mine frightened me. My reflexes snatched my hand away and placed it smoothly in my pocket. She stopped, turned, and cupped my face. "Pete, what's on your mind?" I lowered my eyes, and she lifted my chin. "Am I my father?" She paused a moment, and then smiled. "My love, you are not your father per se. But you are more like him than you know..."

Then she pecked my lips, nose, and forehead. Chuckling she said, "and I love you anyway… I am SOME kind of woman, yes I am!"

No, these people here in the sanctuary had no idea who they were mourning. I was standing in the church that he had labored in all of my life, and most of the congregants and mourners were darker than my wife. Had they any idea who had been behind the pulpit in their own church? I was pained when I concluded that his preaching robe had hidden the hateful part of him, and the white sheets had hidden the loving part of him. Who was my father, if all that we had ever known was a veiled imitation? And who was I if I was more like him than I knew? Ruthy's answer to my question earlier was on repeat, and try as I might, I could not find the stop button to ease my thoughts.

*\* \* \**

*That which I hated*
*I have become*
*\* \* \**

# CHAPTER 8

There was no time for hate or weakness… Which meant we had to keep on moving. Ruthy and I ached for time to grieve openly, but that time never seemed to come. The day after the killings, our mothers didn't just come together to raise us… They dressed as they always had, dried our tears, and smiled while working for families we knew had always hated us silently.

Oddly, the whiteness of their freshly washed and ironed uniforms was just as perfect as the sheets worn by the hooded white men. Only of course, these broken women cloaked themselves in white that had been soaked in love, scrubbed with stout fear, brightened by their tears, and ironed by the fires that had purified their souls. The men on the other hand had draped themselves in sheets soaked with hate, washed by jealousy, and stained by the blood of the images of God they persecuted. White might have symbolized purity… But it either meant painful humility or the threat of the end of us.

Broken hearted and bogged down with gaping voids that yearned to be fulfilled, Ruthy and I trudged along completing our chores as if nothing happened. Certainly our mothers would have loved to have mourned like others, but this was time that food and bills simply would not afford them. In the midst of our struggle, we were forced to step in and help out.

Here it was July 3, 1960; on the eve of an independence we were not allowed to share in, and we had tended to the chickens, milked the one cow we owned, fed the pigs, done our housework and felt our only glimpse of freedom as we strolled briskly to Pete's house to help our mothers.

My new role at Pete's house was to tend to the yard. Whites expected their grass to be perfectly manicured. Each blade was to be in place and perfectly greened to match the neatly trimmed trees and weeded bushes. Nothing in their neighborhoods was ever out of place. How different was my life from their yards? My life was completely out of order. Death remained in my thoughts and the bitter smell of its company singed the hair in my nostrils. My life, in a matter of moments had become a smathering of fears, questions, and tenacity. No amount of busy work could ease my thoughts though it appeared that my mother was doing her best to occupy the space filled with everything and nothing all at once. I remained busy weeding, planting, and mowing grass that I might never be able to enjoy. Ruthy on the other hand was made to wash, cook, clean, and be the personal help for Pete's sister Jane.

I could see in her eyes the hurt and anger she felt every time Jane commanded her to do something or made her sit for hours to listen to meaningless stories. Ruthy was only 6, but her new role was already eating her alive. Still we remained silent, and remained strong as we waited on the Lord to renew our strength. We walked that day in the blazing hot sun. We walked, but did not faint.

\* \* \*

*That which I feared*
*I came from*
\* \* \*

# CHAPTER 9

I remained in town with my wife and grandchildren until we were able to meet for the reading of the will. I cannot say that I was excited, in fact I was certain that my father had left me little to nothing… He had put his hope in me, and it appeared that I was his biggest disappointment. Aside from me spreading the gospel of Jesus Christ, there was nothing I had done to please him. Somehow, despite heeding my call to preach just as my father had, he remained disappointed in me. My decision to remain in Shubuta came only out of obligation to my siblings, who each reminded me that our parents had taught me to respect my elders, and the wishes of the dead. So, as much as it pained me, and as uncomfortable as it made my wife, we remained there so that I might respect my fathers wishes. That might have been the only thing I had ever done in my adult life that pleased him, so I took what comfort I could in feeling like I'd finally made him smile. Though my wife cringed at the idea of remaining in this town for a single second, she loved me enough to let me put my past to rest before we returned to our lives. Our lives might have been full of struggle, but outside of this town we struggled together and we were safe loving each other.

The reading of my fathers will proved to be a terrifyingly satisfying experience. Here I was, sitting in a room with my siblings who were just as much strangers as they were blood relatives; waiting for the lawyer who as a child I'd accused of not giving me enough candy for my penny, to read the wishes of the man who had once been my everything and had then stolen my everything in the heat of the moment. My fingers tingled with anxiety, and my legs bounced up and down nervously with the force of calve muscles that had strengthened and toned in the aftermath of two-mile walks to school. I glanced over at my beautiful wife, knowing that no matter what I walked away with, I would still walk away with her heart. She smiled and I almost lost myself in the midst of the brilliant brown abyss her eyes held, when the lawyer cleared his throat and rolled his own eyes.

Her eyes darted first to him, then to the ground. I nudged her silently, she did not need to lower her eyes… I'd make sure of that. She brought her eyes back up to mine, smiled coyly as only she could, and then raised them to meet the eyes of the attorney who glared at her with a look that radiated with contrite hatred. She stared back, through him almost… Hearing apologies she'd never received but was always entitled to, seeing somewhere in him the image of God and resonating on her longing to love God and his image. My wife smiled and then settled back into her chair. I loved her, she was the peace in the storm, she always had been. She was my testimony to the grace of God. I didn't deserve her. I knew it at that moment, but I'd known it the moment I met her. I looked to Mr. James, my father's attorney, and nodded my head. I was ready for the reading to begin so I could go back to to my home and meet God in my secret place. Repentance was in order.

Ignoring my polite plea to begin the process, he turned to my brothers Dave and Rich, "I don't want to rush you, when you're ready to begin just call my secretary."

We all read between the lines. Dave and Rich glanced at each other knowing full well what he was really saying. Rich being the older of the two looked to each of us, "actually we've been waiting on you."

"Well typically these readings are reserved for immediate family only." He glanced at my wife and I nervously, then shifted to one leg. "Oh, you mean Pete and Ruthy? They about as close to immediate as it comes." Dave replied with genuine irritation. Granted, Dave had not been crazy about my decision to marry Ruthy, but if he wanted me around he had to respect her. He knew this and accepted it. But when he met and married his own wife Elizabeth who was just brown enough to make people tilt their heads confused, the tension dissipated and he came to love my Ruthy. Rich, all these years later thought we both should have chosen better wives… women better suited for us. But when we discovered that he, like my grandfather, had fathered a black child outside of his white marriage, his opinion lost all merit.

Mr. James sighed as if he was speaking another language no one on the planet understood. "Well its not Peter I'm… Ummmm… Would you like to wait…?" We all stared at him with blank disdain and he began again, this time addressing my younger sisters and brother. "I don't think your grandfather would have wanted-"

"We ain't reading my grandfathers will. We here 'bout my daddy. Now, I can't say I'm excited about how dark my brothers like their women," my sister Suzie chimed in and then rolled her eyes as she glared at Ruthy. The others either chuckled nervously or buried their faces in embarrassment. I squeezed Ruthy's hand and she maintained her resolve. Suzie carried on, "Some people ought to just… stay on their side of the tracks. BUT Pete married her, she's here, and we want you to do your job and read this will. I have things to do today, and those things don't involve me sitting here on my hind parts waiting on you to do what my daddy paid you for. I would suggest you focus on that Nigger loving daughter of yours, and get your nose out of Pete's business long enough to deserve the check my daddy paid you. Now... Do you care to get this thing started, or should I continue myself?!" Shocked at her frankness, Mr. James stepped back and cleared his throat. He slowly drew a folded green kerchief from his pocket and dabbed the mounting sweat beads from his pale forehead. He excused himself a moment as we chuckled at Suzie's attitude, which matched perfectly with her more strawberry than blonde hair. In less than sixty seconds, he emerged from the silent hallway with a folder containing my fathers dying wishes.

I can only imagine what was going through everyone else's minds, but my own was completely overwhelmed. I didn't want anything my father had to offer me, he'd stolen the only hero I'd ever known; and no matter what he left me it wouldn't restore that loss. It was because of him that my real life Superman had become my kryptonite. My faith had been crippled and though I knew Ruthy and I greatly loved each other, I also understood that my behavior had possibly caused her to question my love. It was a make or break occurrence, and had it not have been for the God in whom I'd put all of my hope when there was no hope left in humanity, it wouldn't have just broken me. It would have completely broken me down. Ruthy released my hand and patted my knee gently knowing only avenues in the land being traveled by my mind. My God, how I loved this woman.

Mr. James broke the sealed envelope and reluctantly began reading the letter my father had drafted six months before his death.

*"My dear children, I have loved the 8 of you with everything in me. Although I'm sure it didn't always seem that way, I can say with no regrets that I gave you my all, through my life, and now through my death I leave you with all I had. And at this, I cry because you deserve more than I ever had to offer. Richard, my eldest son, you worked your entire life to please your mother and me. You were my prize, and I'm sorry that we held you back from your dreams, your passions, and the love of your life. It's never too late to train horses. I leave you 3 shares of the money I put aside for you all, and all that I have in the barn. Please use everything to chase your dreams. I kept you in a box all of these years, and I'm in a box now... This family can only afford one box at a time."*

We all looked over to Rich who cried silently as he stared out of the room's only window. He blinked non-stop, as if it helped him to maintain his tightly wound desires. His heart was in his tears, and all we could do was watch it fall to pieces making its way to the edges of his chin. Ruthy stood and took him the tissue she'd brought with her. He pulled several pieces and fell into her grasp. "I'm sorry," he said barely above a whisper. Suzie appeared angry, but said nothing, knowing that her silent dismay was more than enough.

*"Dave, my second son. You are the very definition of a man. Thank you. I don't think I need to say why, but I will say that I owe you my life. And though we never spoke of it, I never forgot it. Your mother was always proud of you, even before you went away to school and showed us that you could take care of yourself. I never told you that I loved you son, but I love you. To you, I leave my car which I know you've always wanted, and 6 of the 18 acres of timber. I gave you Rich's share so that he didn't have to feel tied down to it,*

*I know you'll do right by him. Jane, my dearest daughter,
you always were a special child. Whenever you had your eyes on
something, you accomplished it. Yes, I wanted a boy, but God knew
better and gave me what I needed. I know where you have your eyes
pointed now, and I'm pleading with you not to go through with it.
And if you've already crossed the line, please know that I still love you
but for the first time I am disappointed in you. If you're determined
enough to set your eyes in a better direction, one that won't destroy
your heart, faith, and potentially this family, the farm is yours. Until
then, the farm is to be left to Pete. The same thing goes for Suzie and
Earl. You two have long since broken my heart. I had hoped that my
legacy would die with me, but you've passionately chosen to carry
it on. I wanted something different for you two, something better...
Please don't make the same mistakes I've made. You are fighting a
losing battle that would bring nothing but guilt and harm, even if
you could win it. If you allow yourself to give your anger over to God
and experience true freedom and power, you two may split the 12
remaining acres of timber.*

*And to Peter my dear son, I'm sure it seems I've forgotten about
you, but I assure you I have not.*

*First, I must apologize, I don't believe I ever had the chance to
ask your forgiveness... but I'm sorry for the way I treated you. I love
you son, and Ruthy too. Ever since you left the house 35 years ago, I've
desired your forgiveness and am only beginning to forgive myself.
You showed me what it means to follow God even if it means leaving
behind everything the world tries to offer. You won't know what this
means, but you gave me the courage to seek after God in a way I never
thought possible. Thank you. And thank Ruthy, she is just as brave
and beautifully formed as you were. My pride and joy are your resolve
to know God for yourself, and love others because of who you know
God to be. For that reason,*

*I have left you the house, and farmland, 2 shares of the money, all of the homes we've been renting out... And I hope you will take over at Sufficient Grace. My deacons and the board know my decision. Please consider my wishes. Things are different now, but it takes a man like you to to keep things here changing for the better. I trust in God, and know you'll do right by your brothers and sisters. I left you what I took from you when you left home... everything.*

*The last thing I have to say will hurt all of you, but I can hide it no longer. At the beginning of this letter I said 8 children, but there are only 6 of you here. Because f my unwise decisions there are two siblings you have never had the chance to meet. If you desire to meet them, you will find their names and pictures in a box in the attic. The remaining money, land, and the Laundromat will go to them. I did not do right by them while I lived, and they knew me largely at a distance. While you may feel cheated, they deserve something good from the man they never got to know as their fulltime father."*

\* \* \*

*That which hurt me*
*Has taken me over*
*That which abandoned me*
*Is also my cover*

\* \* \*

# CHAPTER 10

There was not a person in our small town who hadn't known about Pete Sr. He was not a bad person necessarily, but he was what I liked to call "the root of the problem." Pete Sr. was just going along to get along. His indiscretions had apparently only been a secret to Pete. There was that irony again; Pete Sr. wore sheets and Pete Jr. wore blinders.

There were days that the thought of Pete Sr. made me sick to my stomach. On those days I could barely comprehend how God had allowed such a strong desire to fester within Ruthy. How could she love the man whose father had helped murder her own? It wasn't Pete Jr.'s fault, but there was absolutely no way I could do it. If forgiveness and salvation had meant marrying Jane or Suzie, I would've probably chosen to travel to hell a thousand times over.

Thankfully, that had never been my burden to bare. I never blurred the lines between us and them. I knew how to play the fence; and though I genuinely believed that Pete Jr. cared about us, navigating our friendship was a lifelong battle I felt myself fighting regularly. I never openly questioned the marriage between Pete and Ruthy, I knew their love was genuine. But when I saw them together I had to pray my questions away at times so that I wouldn't ruin something that was so mysteriously beautiful, that only God could have put it together.

The one good thing that I could say about Pete Sr. was that after our fathers were murdered, he had not only given Ruthy and I jobs to help our family out, but he was careful to assure that we had basic protections. My parents had not owned their land, and though we moved in with Ruthy and her mom, we barely had enough most days to eat. After the murder, my mother had to leave her job as a nurse at the black clinic. It seemed that my fathers death struck an awareness in other employees and patients who were now afraid that the hooded men might hurt them for allowing her to stay. Perhaps they were afraid that she would maintain my father's work advocating for basic human and civil rights. Either way, she was forced out of the clinic and into work as a maid. She was able to take in small amounts of money by doing laundry for local white families, and selling some of the preserves that she was able to can. The struggle was more than real, it was non stop.

Needless to say, we struggled to pull enough together to pay the yearly taxes. Pete Sr. paid the taxes on our family land for more than 5 years. I could tell that hatred wasn't who he was, which meant that he had an internal battle raging that was just as deep as my own. In retrospect it was so much more than an internal battle; it was genuine fear. Twice Pete Sr. had decided to walk away from his klan family, and twice they had literally lit a fire in his home. Maybe it was his guilt that drove him to be so kind. But one thing was for sure, he saw to it that no matter how we struggled, we never went without. I just wish his voice had have been as bold as his actions.

*** *

*I became my father
By no fault of my own*
*** *

# CHAPTER 11

After the reading of the will, I cried uncontrollably. Usually my tears might have dried at some point, but even the worried stares of my grandchildren and the hushed coo's of comfort coming from my wife brought me the least bit of relief. I was mourning the loss of my father. He was the only man who'd carried the pleasure of building me up and the burden of tearing me down. No one else had been so crass as to try, but even if they had, I was too busy overcompensating for my brokenness to have let them succeed. My heart and soul knew that the Lord was my shepherd, but my mind told me that the world would eat me alive if I gave God full control.

I felt myself being overtaken by grief, but fulfilled by the freedom of forgiveness. I had been carrying the weight of my father's actions, and he had been carrying them in his own pack of burdens. How I wished I had at least been able to extend him the forgiveness he so desired. Had I not been so caught up in my anger, I might have… called, visited, done something other than sending an obligatory postcard void of a return address to let him know that I was alive. In the same way that he carried his guilt for the rest of his life, I would wear the weight of his death as the painfully drab garb that it was. I had forgiven him… Too little too late. Could I ever forgive myself? Only time would tell. I silently prayed that God would deliver me from this centrifuge of self loathing.

One thing was for certain, running away was no longer an option. I needed to collect myself and do it quickly. Then and only then could I consider how my wife and children were feeling. And perhaps there was something I could do to rid myself of the vicissitudes of my stomach. Deep inside I knew that God wanted me to yield to my father's wishes and preach the gospel in Shubuta, but my flesh crawled at the thought. Painfully sick to my stomach, I remained tightly coiled in the fetal position for three days. I can't say what brought me back to reality, but the sound of her voice led me to roll over and rediscover her soft beauty. It was the first time I'd moved since hearing my fathers last wishes. My eyes suddenly noticed the gray and blue striped sheets provided by my childhood home, and were just as quickly appalled by the stark white walls that seemed to close us in from the carefree world.

"I see your body still works… That's a good sign." She sat next to me, and stretched her legs while raising my head into her lap. I met her eyes and the comfort I had always needed received my brokenness. "The kids are with Dave. He wanted to spend some time with them, and I thought we needed to be alone." She stroked my hairline, just above my right ear. "My mother used to do that," I said, "when I'd had a rough day at school she'd lay me on her lap and rub there. I loved when she did that… I miss her… I miss my father… and after three days of searching for peace, I miss you." I puckered up for a kiss, but she turned up her nose in playful disgust.

Hitting my forehead with the palm of her hand she chuckled and said, "Now you know how bad your breath stinks! I married a man, not a dragon." I chuckled and sat up slowly, realizing that the tears I'd cried had come at a physical cost. I was weak, sore, and starving. Before I could ask, Ruthy opened a bag that smelled of greasy tastiness. "You always did love the burgers at our favorite spot. After you wash up, and I air this room out, we'll eat." "I love you." Tears threatened to fall again. Relieved at the small glimpse of the Peter she'd fallen in love with she replied, "I love you more." "I love you three." She hated when I said that, but as always she responded warmly, "I love you four." We burst into laughter and then she held up her hand. Refusing to breathe in, she ran to the door and opened it as if the room were on fire. Only she could turn such a dreary moment into joyful laughter. I was confused until she threw her head out of the opened door and panted like a pup in need of water. I raised my arms, smelling the sour must underneath. "Come here, you need a hug," I said and she squealed like she was 17 again.

"Fine, fine… I'll take a shower-"

"A long… hot shower… with lots of soap?"

"Yes, with lots of soap. But this, this right here," I said as I fanned the smell toward her, "This is all man! Yup, this is all man. Look all grossed out if you want to," I walked away calling over my shoulder, "but you know you want this!" She laughed, as did I. And though the gnawing in my gut remained, the peace in the moment was more than enough to calm my spirit. Hopefully with a fresh bar of ivory soap, I could wash the gnawing feeling away permanently.

*\* \* \**

*I became my father*
*And my, how my soul has grown*
*\* \* \**

# CHAPTER 12

Having finally talked me off the emotional ledge from which I had refused to budge for the better part of a week, Ruthy felt better returning home. She had insisted on staying with me as I went through my parents home and cleaned things out. We both wanted to return to Denver for good, but somewhere in my soul I yearned to please my father. The grandchildren were out of school for the summer, and I pleaded with her to let them get back to normalcy.

Certainly they missed their friends and their time swimming at Congress Park. They took swimming lessons there three times a week, and on occasion, Ruthy would find a seat just inside the gates and recline while they enjoyed free swim time. She carried bags of snacks, and they would hop out of the pool to grab a quick snack, only to race back to the water. I never understood how Ruthy had enough patience to put up with the screaming, laughter, and constant whistling of life guards. It was not until one afternoon when she talked me into coming along that I understood why she loved to take them swimming. On this particular day, the children dragged me into the pool insisting that I ought not be ashamed of my powder white skin. I removed my shirt, slipped into the water, and laughed until my soul couldn't stand any more joy.

When we got out of the pool for snacks, I noticed she wore her favorite leopard print shades. Snapping my fingers repeatedly in front of her face, with no response, I realized that Ruthy was asleep. The sun had kissed her melanin and caressed her with full and complete relaxation. Ruthy carried the responsibility of being responsible for everything and everybody. She was exhausted, and Congress Park pool gave her space to doze off to the joyous sound of her grandchildren's raucous laughter.

Despite the calming feeling the pools waves gave her, Ruthy was determined not to abandon me in my time of need. She chose to go to her mother's home in Hazlehurst and enjoy a different type of rest. The children had always felt a special freedom there in Hazlehurst. Few questions about their heritage, complete love from Ruthy's mother and Aunt, and enough country land that they could run and play without fear. I bathed in the unconditional love Ruthy's mom had given me, and she loved my children even more.

Knowing that Ruthy would be gone and safe, I began preparing myself for what other secrets I might uncover as I cleared out the house. My siblings had offered to come help, but I wanted to be alone. I didn't want anyone to know my fathers secret, and I certainly didn't want anyone to see me cry if I discovered more than I wanted to know. I kissed my wife and grandchildren goodbye, knowing that I might not be the same man when they saw me again. What did the future hold? I didn't know, but I did know that my future held the secrets of my fathers past, and the pain of my present discoveries.

Having kissed the last of my three grandchildren and seated them in the cars back seat, I reminded my wife exactly how much I had always loved her. I kissed her with such passion, and held her so close that she hesitated to get into the car.

 "Are you sure you want to do this by yourself? I can leave the kids with Dave." Ruthy's eyes were still closed when she asked. I reached around her, and opened the door. Without opening her eyes, she sucked her teeth at my gesture. "Peter, you are some kind of special. Do you know how many men wish they had this kind of support?" I felt bad, but I needed to do this on my own. There was no way that I could ever love her fully and completely if her love was a mere crutch. I kissed her again, this time gazing in to her eyes. "And all they will ever have the chance to do is wish. Call me when you get to your mom's." She told me she loved me, and waved as she rolled away.

*  *  *

*I resisted the mirrors before me*
*Desiring not to know the truth*
*I shielded my eyes from the light*
*Denying the realness of proof*

*  *  *

# CHAPTER 13

The house that held such beautiful memories held me captive to the truths that lurked inside it. "Lord, still my soul, and bring rest to my mind. Allow me only to discover what you desire, that it might be used to your glory. Thank you… In Jesus name, Amen." Ordinarily my prayers were inner mumbles only to be understood by God, but today as I unearthed my fathers truth, I removed my voice from the rubble. I turned the doors deadbolt lock, took a deep breath and slowly made my way to the attic. My hearts racing could only be measured against the low creek of the stairs. My hands shook, and then I reached the attic door. This room held secrets, accomplishments, heirlooms, gifts, and things I couldn't put a name to. What might this room hold for me?

When I finally convinced myself to open the door and step inside, my eyes were met by moist walls lined with boxes. Some boxes were labeled with our names and overflowed with awards, baby blankets, and stuffed animals. My eyes searched the box lined perimeter for my own name. My name, Pete, stared back at me across the room and I elected to lessen the space that separated us. Excited for what I might find, I lifted its top and searched its contents with my brown eyes. My lettermans jacket fit just like it had when I'd worn it in high school.

Trophies that were now covered with dust had once shined in the light of the sun, and small posters of women and superheroes littered the boxes bottom. Breathing in the dank attic air kept me grounded in the moment, as my mind took brief walks down memory lane. This box held evidence that an old me had once existed. Who else would've owned collectible baseball cards, fishing hooks and bobs, and a set of boxing gloves? Caught off guard by the sight of something I thought I'd never see again, I grabbed my chest in excitement. Jr., the light green teddy bear Ruthy had given me on my 13th birthday peered out. Around his neck was my mothers golden necklace; a locket holding my baby pictures and her warm smile. His head was covered by the baby ball cap that had been my fathers gift to me on my 2nd birthday. I pulled Jr. from the box holding him close to my heart. How did Ruthy do it? She was here for me even when she wasn't here with me. Suddenly feeling comforted, I sat Jr. in the window sill to watch as I tackled the tremendous task ahead.

Most boxes in the room were labeled, so I tackled them first. Looking through each box that held momentos from our childhoods, I pulled out things that didn't belong, put them in the correct box and carried it downstairs near the front door. I cried every time I opened a box that held something of my mothers. She had been the first woman I'd loved, and the woman I'd fallen in love with was more like her than I had ever understood. My eyes pooled with tears streaming silently, and then they were made to rest on a photograph of my mother wearing the yellow sundress I adored, cream sandals, and a matching large brimmed hat. The wind must have been blowing, because even in the photograph it was clear that her long brown hair had taken flight and the corners of her dress had followed suit. How beautiful was she, just standing in the sun, holding her hat with one hand and her own shoulder with the other? Within moments, I found myself sitting Indian style in the center of the floor surrounded by photographs. Deep sadness overtook my heart, but relief that she had not suffered in her death calmed me… I'd forgotten how much I missed my mother.

I had been consumed with my thoughts so long that I never heard the front door open and close, I hadn't heard Dave and Rich climb the stairs, and I never saw them sit next to me and cry like babies. When we collected ourselves, I hugged them both and asked why they had come. Rich looked nervously at Dave, and Dave spoke up, "Uhhh… Well we, we just wanted to support you… Right Rich?" Rich nodded anxiously and began searching the room for somewhere to begin. As much as I had desperately wanted to be alone, I was extremely relieved that they had come to join me. Not understanding their sudden willingness to help, or their nervous glances, I told them what my system was and we went to work.

A few hours later, we had finished all of the boxes with labels. We agreed to get some lunch and then get back to work. When I picked up my phone, I had a missed call from Ruthy. Upset because I had missed the chance to hear the sound of her voice, I left the room to return her call, but she didn't answer. I waited a few minutes and then called again. She had reached her mothers house in Hazlehurst and was feeding the children. Satisfied that they were safe and settled in, I returned to the attic. "Alright guys, who's ready for-" I stopped dead in my tracks as I saw them shuffling through two open boxes. Dave hissed, "its not in here!" Before Rich could respond I spoke up "what's not in there?" They both turned immediately and said nothing. "What's up guys? Maybe I can help you find it."

Aware that something was going on I decided to play stupid like I had learned to do with my children. "Oh, we" Rich held the E like a blues singer, "were just looking for umm… for dad's old marked up Bible. It was his favorite ya know?" I chuckled, "Its downstairs on dad's nightstand. Funny thing is, its open to Exodus 20, blew me away when I looked over and saw it there." I grabbed the broom and began to sweep. Appearing a bit calm Dave spoke up excitedly, "Well… I'm still hungry, whose up for some burgers?!" I agreed and then told them I was tired and wanted to check in with Ruthy again because I was missing her so much. Reluctantly they went without me, and I made myself momentarily comfortable.

\* \* \*

*I blamed him for what I felt*
*Forgetting that I came forth from his seed*
\* \* \*

# CHAPTER 14

"**P**ete, do you remember Mr. Asberry?" I had been racking my mind for months, trying to find a way to pull Pete completely out of his fog. It seemed like every time I made an attempt to help things, something happened that pushed him back into his struggle. "Yeah… Why?" His response was a bit sharper than I had expected, so I took a moment to collect myself before continuing. Having taken a deep breath I said simply, "he's the reason I married you." A slight scowl spread across his face and I could tell that what I'd said had both stung and intrigued him. The distance in his eyes was filled only by the questions lingering behind his pupils. His tongue ceased to strike back the way I could feel he wanted to. "What did you just say?" "I said that Mr. Asberry was the reason I married you." Just as he was about to return my honesty with a flippant remark, I stared at him with eyes that demanded absolute silence and abruptly thrust my hand into his face. I was officially tired of who he had become. His lips parted to protest my frustration but I shook my head sharply and spoke, "You heard me correctly. Have a seat so I can explain something to you. Don't speak, just listen."

Absentmindedly, Peter fell into the seat directly behind him. His pale white forearms were like midnight lightning bugs, against the backdrop of the charcoal lazy boy chair. Shrinking away like a shamed child for the first time since his parents had sent him away years ago, Peter closed his eyes and braced for a verbal lashing. Sitting lightly on the wooden coffee table, I placed my hands on his knees and squeezed lightly. Nestling my knees just between his, I braced myself to offer my husband a bitter dose of needed truth.

"Peter, I fell in love with you that night. I saw fight in you that night, I saw a special spark in your eyes. It was like God made you privy to a vision the rest of us were not. You dreamed big, you saw truth, you… knew who you were." Until that moment, Peter's eyes had been closed lazily. As I spoke, he squeezed his eyes tight as if he were squeezing my words from his ears. I can't say what soothed him, but his eyes opened briefly when I said that he knew who he was. He smiled gingerly, and just when I relaxed, thinking I had made some headway, his eyes welled up with tears and he seemingly released the only bit of fight he still held in a single scratchy breath. "I didn't know anything I thought I did… but it was a fluke. He lost his life, and I could have stopped it. If I knew even half as much as I thought I did, I could have stopped a lot of things… but I didn't, I'm just as guilty as my-"

"Your what?!" I demanded to know what guilt he'd been carrying all this time that had finally become too heavy for his pale soul. True to form, Peter didn't answer my question. I searched his eyes for signs of desired confession. My eyes failed me, but Pete's eyes boasted of the truths he had just discovered. Truths I'd learned years ago while helping my mother hang freshly washed linens. I'd come to know the secrets of the skin that lay beneath the starched white sheets I'd scrubbed by hand. For a moment, I lost myself in terrifying memories as I recalled how long I'd scrubbed and treated the blood stained sheets before they'd finally come clean. Peroxide, and baking soda eventually aided me in removing the blood spots.

I'd complained, "Momma! Pete's mom must be on the rag, you should've seen how much blood was on them sheets! What a nasty woman." Staring deep into my eyes, she snatched me close until the warmth of her breath poured into my ear and melted the words germinating in my throat to the degree that only a small gasp escaped me. A shaky, "Yes'm?" was all I could muster after the gulp cleared my esophagus.

"Look closely at them sheets baby. Them ain't no regular sheets. LOOK AT EM!" she demanded. It was only then that I examined the sheets and noticed the small emblem hand stitched onto the other side. I looked intently at her, "Noooo, Mama. Ain't no way that mean what I think it mean, Mama!"

"Hush child!"

"But Mamma, last night… at the church, are you saying?"

"Keep yo' voice down girl," She scanned the house and surrounding trees as she whispered harshly. "It means exactly wachu think. Pete's daddy is one of them, and his grandpa is too. I would be surprised if one day…"

She watched questions, confusion, and fear take me over.

"Pete? Jane?"

"Pete don't know a thing, I don't know about the others. But you keep yo' mouth shut, we ain't posed' to know nuthin'."

When I felt the first tear drop navigate its way from the corners of my eyes to the bend of my lips, I left my secrets and came back to Pete, my husband. He knew. I looked at him lovingly. "Ruthy baby, I remember Mr. Asberry. And I keep trying to forget that night, but sometimes I remember it.

Why did it have to happen? To him? I should've stopped it, I could've stopped it." I didn't find out until much later exactly what Pete meant.

*I blamed him for fatherly heartbreak*
*But it is brokenness that I need*

# CHAPTER 15

Blacks and whites didn't much worship together. And the few blacks that managed to somehow come to white churches were either caregivers for white families and had to wait on the family, or had to sit in sweltering cars and wait for the families they drove. Even the wealthy blacks didn't dare try to go to white churches, and by 1970, southern blacks had opened their own churches and stood clear of white folks on Sundays. For southern blacks, the white church meant one of two things. Either a front for the White Knights of the Klu Klux Klan who somehow believed that vigilante murders were kingdom work, or it meant an unusually sympathetic ear that could neither conceive of experience nor fully comprehend the struggle but at least saw the image of God in skin the color of daybreak.

Mr. Asberry was a white Christian like no other. Shubuta had never seen a man like him, and I don't know if the kingdom of God ever had either. He believed firmly that churches ought not be segregated, and he boldly told people so

"The gospel is the same in their church as it is here. At least it should be! If Jesus was who he said he was he'd be angry about what goes on every Sunday." It seemed like such a simple thing to say, but it was also very dangerous. We didn't mix and that was just the way it was. It wasn't a written rule anymore, it was unspoken but it was the rule. Dejure segregation, the legal kind, had separated us all in every possible physical way. Even as laws changed de facto segregation was preferred by the ruling majority, and the rest of us followed suit so that we could stay alive. Though we all knew the truth on some level, no one dared speak what they secretly thought they knew. Mr. Asberry dared to live the loving gospel we so innately preached about, while quietly hating his creation.

Because of his convictions, Mr. Asberry did the most insane thing I had ever seen. He began a small youth bible study and instead of screaming about why segregation was biblical, he taught us about Jesus and why he was so mercilessly persecuted. Never before had I conceived of a savior who'd lived a life dedicated to love all, and then gave his own life to bring salvation to all who would receive it. My father hadn't actually told me to hate blacks, but he never seemed particularly upset when my grandfather did. We were good to Ruthy and her mother Esther. But was being good to them good enough, or did God require more of my faith and more of me? Mr. Asberry challenged us to ask these questions until we had better cause for our answers than, "that's how its always been and that's how its always gonna be." He would say, "don't just know and believe. Know why you believe."

Parents were already bothered at this contention that Jesus loved everyone equally, and that according to Paul we were all the same in Christ. Nigger lover whispers and eyes ablaze with disrupted fear never seemed to bother him though. In fact, he saw some people questioning their hatred because of his teaching and that fueled his fire. It wasn't until my grandfather, our pastor, discovered that we'd begun to have a mixed bible study that I discovered how deep blind hatred ran in Shubuta.

*  *  *

*I became my father*
*When I came to know Christ*
*I became my father*
*When I fell to my knees that night*
*  *  *

# CHAPTER 16

P eter had been raving about this deacon at his church. I didn't tell Peter, but I'd already heard about Mr. Asberry and how stirred up he was getting people around town. There was a black woman down the road from us and Mr. Asberry loved her. She loved him too but she understood that nothing could come of their feelings. It was one thing for a white man to have a Black woman on the side even though he was married. It was something completely different for a white man to fall in love with a black woman and commit himself to her. Mr. Asberry had vowed his love to her, Olivia. He never married another woman because he didn't want to disrespect her or the way he felt about her. Instead, he just made frequent visits to her home, and they loved each other in the shadows. Whites knew about his visits, but didn't know how deep their feelings ran. If they ever found out he would do much more than cause a stir

Whites were not happy about whatever he was teaching at the church, but Pete wasn't like the rest of them. Mr Asberry had brought him to the same conclusion that blacks had long since reached; the royal law is the law of love, and you don't get to pick and choose which of God's people you love. Seeing the sudden consciousness Pete had, I can't say that I was completely surprised when he asked me to come to church with him.

I was folding clothes one breezy April afternoon. I hated having to do it, but Momma didn't believe in laziness, and Pete's mom and dad would give me $2.00 a week. At 15, I thought I was rich. On this particular day I was on the porch alone folding clothes and singing my favorite song to myself, Jesus be a fence. "Hey Ruthy!" I turned my head just in time to feel Pete slip his hands along my waistline. I smiled loving the attention, then suddenly realizing that someone might uncover our young affection, I pulled away. "No one is here but us. Your mother is at the market and my father is at the church."

"But Peter what if-"

"Don't worry, we're safe."

I hesitated, but yielded nonetheless. I came to face Pete and hugged him deeply, then stepped back to drink in the moment I felt in his eyes. "Busted." We both turned knowing the trouble we were in. Zeke grinned mischievously as we sighed from relief. He'd come through the back porch quietly and watched the whole scene through the shielding screen. I shot Pete a knowing glance and tearfully cast my eyes to the wooden floor beneath me. Folding kept my fingers too busy to wrap them around Pete and Zekes necks and squeeze until my hidden desires lost their zeal for life. Zeke chuckled, "Ruthy, Pete told me a long time ago. I'm not crazy about you two but, I won't tell if you won't. Ya'll just better be more careful about things. Better be glad I was the only one who saw."

"No, I saw too, and I'm telling Momma and Daddy! Pete, this nig-" Peters sister Jane filled the doorway leading to the kitchen. "Don't... you... dare!"

Pete balled his fists, "You don't have to like it, but you keep your mouth shut!" Jane left abruptly, and I secretly hoped this was enough for her never to speak to me again.

Being her friend and maid was a burden I was painfully tired of carrying. I heard her bedroom door slam and knew that not only did she hate me, but that her anger put Zeke and I both in danger. I hurriedly folded the last few items and turned to put the basket away. "Ruthy, Zeke wait. I wanted to talk to you both." "Pete, now isn't a good time. We better get on home before it starts getting dark."

"Wait. I was wondering if ya'll would come to church with me."

"No thanks Pete, we do our own churching," I said. "Mr. Asberry is different you guys. I told him about you two and he wants you to come. Other Negroes come too! Please?!"

"Pete, you tryna get me killed?" Zeke said gruffly. "This here… you two is bad enough, but you know Righteous Remnant don't do Negroes."

"I promise it'll be okay. Cross my heart." Pause… He motioned, "hope to die…" He paused again waiting as Zeke and I stared at each other in disbelief.

You just didn't tell a white man no, and you certainly didn't go to their churches. The last time I'd heard of something like that, white folks gathered at the Chickasawhay River hanging bridge and celebrated the Negro hanging near the Lakes weeping trees. "Stick a needle," pause…

But you never told a white man no, even if he said he'd love and protect you, and even if he stole your innocence. No, meant death.

"Ok Pete fine." Zeke looked at me as I spoke, "Ruthy are you crazy?!" I opened my mouth to respond and Pete spoke up. "It'll be great, I'll talk to your moms. Don't worry, what's the worse that could happen?" "Negroes never get to ask that question. Breathing is the worse that can happen. Ruthy let's go. NOW!" I smiled nervously at Pete and left without another word.

*             *             *

"So you guys, what did you think about bible study?"

"Honestly Pete, I've never met a more genuine white man-" Zeke interrupted me, giving me a look that told me he didn't trust any ears that might be hovering nearby. "What she meant was that he taught us a lot."

"Zeke, ain't nobody paying us attention. We're all believers here, and God created us the same. Didn't you hear Mr. Asberry?" Pete responded excitedly.

"Well yes we did."

Just as Zeke slowed his head from its nodding motion, we were confronted by the very men who had terrified my dreams since the night our fathers were brutally murdered. "Wachu say nigger?" Zeke replied simply, "I said yas'suh."

"Yas'suh who?" the voice shot back. Without hesitation I chimed in, "yas'suh Mr. Pete sir." Peter looked mortified, but he'd learned long ago never to interrupt because it could only make matters much worse. Literally shaking, we stood in still silence finding comfort only in the breath of God as it blew warm breeze through the trees surrounding our fear. I prayed silently that God would spare us, and swore I'd never stray if he'd only protect us. Fear had masterfully chased the words from my lips and for the first time, Zeke's protective demeanor dissipated. Who would be my victor tonight? I'd never been completely dependent on God, but there was a first time for everything.

These men chastised us verbally. To the point that I felt my bladder threaten to overflow with urine composed of all the fear my body desired to release. Just as I became aware that their words would likely become acts that threatened my life and safety, a calm washed over me.

86

Though I was prepared to die and knew on some level that death was imminent, I reached out to squeeze Zeke's hand. I could feel anger rise up in him like I hadn't seen in years. He spoke simply, never taking his eyes from the mystery beneath white sheets. His eyes hungrily roamed the blue expanse of the eyes that peeked out from beneath the cover of the white hood. "Let's go Ruthy." I followed in silence hoping that the still of the night would hold back their wrath.

Quiet winds billowed and I whispered thank you to the ever present and almighty God who'd just spared our lives. "Peter, you better not follow those niggers!" My neck threatened to swivel but when Zeke jerked me forward I had the sudden understanding that turning back could cause me to turn into a pillar of salt. I'd spoil to my own demise. Peter's stammering added tension, "Those are... But they're my... umm, they..."
"All they are is niggers. They're a pair of coons, and they ain't got no place here. Go home niggers!" Zeke's grip tightened and we continued to walk. Pete caught up with us, but aside from our eyes peering from the abyss
of slits made small with an amalgamation of anger, relief, and confusion, our pace did not change.

"They're just kids, they're leaving," I heard the voice of the man who'd called Pete's name say. I couldn't make out what the others were saying to him but their harsh and hushed tones sent me tumbling to the ground at which the men laughed heartily. Scrambling to get back up, Zeke grabbed one arm and Pete grabbed the other. "Don't touch that nigger!" The voice sounded strangely familiar, aged and husky unlike the first man. Pete froze and released my arm immediately.

"Where is God in this?" This voice was tough as nails, but compassionate and soothing. "Mr. Asberry?" Pete posed the question to nobody in particular. All three of us turned in time to see Mr. Asberry making his way through the churches courtyard. The first man's voice pierced the screaming darkness, "Asberry, you stay outta this." Unphased by their anger, Mr. Asberry made his way to us. "You say you're believing people, but you mistreat His beloved children." He reached down and brushed the roads dust from my newly ripped pink skirt. It had always been my favorite.

"Haven't I taught you all better than this? These children who were here, only to worship the very God you say you worship, will now carry this night forever."

"Good, they can carry it right back to their side of town, they don't belong here."

"They don't belong here?!" We could see now that mere concern wasn't all that Mr. Asberry felt. He held this righteous indignation that bled through his appendages, and while his terror was otherwise obvious, tonight his

cup boiled over with a mixture of anger and pity. His hands shook as he pressed his eyes to meet those of the last hidden man who had spoken. "Tell me son, where exactly do THEY belong? Africa?! The place THEY lived contently until we stole them and brought them here? Are they any more strangers to this land than your own German born parents who came here on their own accord? Their family had no choice in the matter and they've been here longer than your family. They are where they belong... Here, working for the kingdom of God. Perhaps it is you who are not where *you* belong."

The gruffy familiar voice who frightened me as much as Pete's grandfather, spoke up, "What exactlly do you mean Asberry?"

Defiantly Mr. Asberry replied, "These children have done nothing to any of you. Let them go home safely and in peace."

He nodded toward us as if to tell us silently that the precious Lord would take our hands and lead us home. Hesitatnly, we walked away remembering Mr. Asberry's lesson about Lot's exit from the land of Sodom and how his wife looked back and turned to a pillar of salt.

Afraid that if I somehow took my eyes off the prize of safety and looked back I'd become my own pillar of salt and spoil the Lords provision for my life, I stared straight ahead assuredly. The silence should have warned us of the storm to come. We were halfway across the dustry road that would guarantee our refuge in the brush and trees God had created in preparation in this moment.

*　*　*

*I became my father*
*Then yielded to God's reign*
*I became my father*
*When I welcomed my pain*

*　*　*

# CHAPTER 17

I thought I heard a deep throated voice tell Mr. Asberry that his days were numbered.

"Man who is born of a woman is but a few days and full of trouble." Mr. Asberry's reply caused me to shiver in the warm spring air. How ironic that Easter Sunday was less than five days away and Mr. Asberry was about to allow himself to be sacrificed. The hooded men argued among themselves. Some felt like they should just leave well enough alone, but most of them were tired of him. When one of them said, "Its bad enough he's messing with that black girl. Now he's teaching these kids it's ok to mix! He's the thorn in my side!" I knew Mr. Asberry was in serious trouble. The hooded man who'd called out to Peter spoke up and tried to calm the others, but there was no calming the things that unfolded.

It was like something had taken over Mr. Asberry and he refused to back down. I continued walking with Zeke though we moved as slow as snails. Despite my good sense, I halted when I heard running and turned to see what was going on. I hoped that the men were running to their trucks to disappear into the April darkness as I'd known them to do. Instead, I saw that Mr. Asberry had knelt to pray, just in front of the men and one of them was racing from the truck with a lengthy 2x4 in hand.

Seemingly unaware of the danger his life was in, he prayed unceasingly. "Lord, open their eyes and show them the hate in their hearts, and the error of their ways. Forgive them Father for they know not what they do or how ignorant they are."

Just as the man neared Mr. Aberry, Zeke screamed. "No!" At the same time that the cloaked man slowed his steps, Mr. Asberry's prayer reached the ear of God. "You opened their eyes when Elisha prayed, and you are still the same God today. Open their eyes today that they might see your angels surrounding me." It was when he said these words that the man attempted to swing the 2x4 at Mr. Asberry's head. Many of the others jeered but the sight quickly quieted their laughter. The wood hit mere air and splintered against the soft breeze. Their lips silenced immediately and the man who'd tried to hit Mr. Asberry yelped out in pain as he fell back on the concrete Ruthy's skirt had been ripped by. Another picked up a splinter attempting to stab Mr. Asberry with it, but somehow while in motion he managed only to impale himself. The men whispered amongst themselves, as did we. An angel stood directly in front of Mr. Asberry, but shielded him on every side. There was no denying what I saw with my own eyes. If I never knew before, I knew that night how real God was.

After a moment or two of awkward silence, the realization that we were still in danger hit us. Knowing they seemingly couldn't harm Mr. Asberry, they returned their attention to us. Though we backed away silently, we hadn't moved far enought fast enough. Our eyes were on the hooded men when we heard laughter and within seconds one of the men had run toward us and snatched Ruthy away. I'll never forget the fear in her eyes and voice. She was powerless as were we. We begged them not to hurt her, but they yanked the ripped part of her skirt until nothing hung but loose strings tethered to her waist line

. Crying, but refusing to beg for innocence they'd stolen when they'd murdered her father, her eyes pleaded on her behalf.

As if her eyes bore a hole through his lids, entering into the secret place where only God had been privy, Mr. Asberry rose, attacking the men ferociously. I saw the story of Sampson come alive, even to the point that this might be his last hurrah. One by one he tossed them aside until Ruthy was the only one standing before him. He then removed his shirt, which had been moistened by sweat and circumstance, and tied it firmly around her waist. It was like he'd taken his perfection and covered her shame, anger, and pain. He wiped her tears away and buried her head against his broad shoulder as he carried her back to Zeke and I. When he placed her gently on the ground, he told me to spend the rest of my life protecting her, and told Zeke that God had called him to do a great work for the kingdom. Then he told us to run and not slow down. He stood slowly as we turned to run into the tree lined forest. He'd barely risen when I yelled out his name. Pow! Footsteps… Pow! Heavy breathing… Pow! Silence…

Though the others appeared to be upset with the cloaked man who had snake like veins, he laughed incredulously encouraging hateful fodder. I looked down down at the clay road, now stained with the blood of an innocent man. I looked defiantly into the cold blue eyes of this… murderer and felt as if my grandfathers hate filled substance stared back. He said something about needing to teach me a lesson, to which I replied simply, that Mr. Asberry had just taught me everything I needed to know. His anger was apparent, but his voice disobeyed his lips. No words escaped the abyss of his hate filled throat.

I stared at Mr. Asberry lying facedown in the clay of the Earth, as blood gushed from the gaping bullet holes in his leg, back, and the nape of his neck. A fierce calm overtook me and I ran to my friends, tugging at their limbs mercilessly. They seemed transfixed by the still air and perhaps flashbacks of their father's deaths.

Having my own father come to mind, I wondered how he might handle this. The man who'd first called my name reminded me of my dad, he didn't seem to want to be there. Whenever he was faced with breakdown events he would say, "Pinch me Pete. Pinch me cuz' this can't be real." Zeke yelped when I pinched. I dug my finger nails in as deep as they'd go, knowing that only a more immediate pain than the one he felt, could snap him back from this nightmare.

Zeke whispered my name. "Pete, we gotta go." Without hesitation, we each grasped Ruthy's wrists and pulled until her feet were forced to follow. We ran into the trees that littered the edge of the dusty road. The three of us ran until dark branches with this colorful moss both faced and followed us.

We ran until our labored breathing drowned out the rhythm of our heavy footsteps and the symphony of leaves being crushed beneath our feet sang to us softly.

We ran until we neither heard nor saw the men whose cowardly white sheets would no doubt invade every dream and moment of peace I'd ever feel. We ran until our feet could take us no further and with safety only a deep breath away, God carried us to our homes.

*  *  *

*I became my father*
*When I knew I wasn't good enough*
*  *  *

# CHAPTER 18

I couldn't believe all that I had seen that night. It seemed that every time I closed my eyes I either saw my father and Zeke's strung up to our favorite climbing tree, or the look in Mr. Asberry's eyes as life escaped him. Just in recalling the story to Pete, I became aware of exactly how emotionally scarred I was because of all the things I had seen. "Pete, I had always loved you, but I married you because you did what Mr. Asberry did that night. You loved me beyond what everyone else thought. You loved me deeper… In a way my father had not been given the chance to." Pete's eyes bashfully met mine,

"I fell in love with you because that night, with Mr. Asberry I saw your faith in God become real and I saw in you a flame that I never thought could be extinguished. My skin was not a barrier between you and me, or between me and God. You taught me that night that my skin was a gateway to your heart and into his hand. I didn't understand what it meant to love yourself until Mr. Asberry allowed those men to take his life because he saw that I was human. He saw that I was inherently valuable, he saw the image of God in me. It was that night that I saw the image of God in you, and I saw both you and Zeke transfigure before my eyes. It was literally like the Spirit of God took you over, you weren't afraid because your trust was completely in Him.

And you trusted him to love you and then you shared that love with me. You could have left me there, you could have walked away from Zeke and I, and there was a moment when I thought you might. But you didn't, you stood by me. You were there with me when my father was murdered and when Mr. Asberry covered my shame and terror with his blood. You understood my pain, and though my skin is a different color, you saw beyond that, and you covered my pain with your tenderness and loyalty. Watching you become a man as convicted and caring as Mr. Asberry has been the biggest blessing God could have ever given me."

"My grandfather shot him." I wasn't surprised at Pete's declaration, I had always known that Pete's grandfather was there that night. Perhaps my reaction was too lifeless because Pete looked at me curiously and then continued. "My father was there too, and so was Mr. James." Stunned at the mention of Mr. James, who I'd always known to dislike black people but never knew to be the cowardly KKK type, I lowered my head and he whispered, "I could have stopped it. I could have stopped all of it."

"Pete, none of that was your fault. You're not responsible for-"

"He killed your father." A pregnant silence filled me, and I couldn't even tell that I had stopped breathing. I did not reply. "Ruthy did you hear me? My father-" before Pete could finish, I cut in.

"Killed my father! And Zekes too!" I screamed it so loud that it even frightened me. Who knew I'd had so much bottled up inside of me? I said nothing for a moment, and Pete continued. "I had no idea they were planning to come that night. I just heard some men yelling and I followed the sounds, I shouldn't have been there... It shouldn't have happened. My momma always used to tell me there was a monster who lived in her bed and I didn't get it; couldn't quite wrap my mind around it, but... ...

What does that make me? Who am I? All those years, I wanted to be just like my father. I watched him take his last breath, and all I could think about was how amazing he had always been to me, and how much I'd hurt him when I chose to marry you. All I could do was trace the veins in his hands. They were the same veins, on the same hands that strung your father up! That is what I wanted to be my entire life. That is who I was trying to impress! A monster, a hypocritical, lying, bastardly monster! I wanted to be a monster, and I never even knew it. What kind of man does that make me?"

"I know Pete."

"What do you know? You're father was not a murderer! He was not a closet racist! He did not kill the father of my best friend and the woman I love! He did NOT employ the very women whose husbands he'd killed. That was NOT your father! All your father was ever guilty of was wearing his humanness and existing. That was his worst crime! He existed, and my father hated him for it." My silence only fueled his fire. In the past when he was angry he asked that I listen silently, it demonstrated my intensity and interest, but today it made him feel desperate and isolated. "Have you heard anything?"

"I hear you Pete,"

"So… Say something, who am I now?"

"The man I fell in love with."

"What does that make me? Hell, what does that make you?"

"It makes you a man with a father he's not proud of."

"All these years and I never knew. I'm so sorry Ruthy, I'm so sorry this is all my fault. I should've known, I should've stopped them. I'm so sorry." Peter sobbed like a baby awaiting a fresh diaper and bottle.

His tears ran furiously down his cheeks like raindrops during a hurricane. The internal rain wouldn't let up and he continued to cry sorrowfully. Finally he caught his breath, and clutching my hand he said, "Please forgive me."
"I don't need to forgive you, it's not your fault." It was apparent that he'd only found out since we'd been back in town for the service but I couldn't figure out how he did. Of course I also didn't quite understanding how he'd never known, but I couldn't ask either question. Now was simply not the time. He needed to clear his conscience and my questions would do him no good.

\* \* \*

*I became my father*
*And I lost the value in stuff*
\* \* \*

# CHAPTER 19

Ruthy had seen me cry before, more times than I could count. She wasn't ashamed of that fact and neither was I. Whoever wrote Amazing Grace must have been writing it with me in mind. Because I suddenly found myself tearfully questioning the very essence of my being… Who was I? What had I wanted to become? What kind of man was I that I couldn't see beyond my fathers façade, and that I loved this monster so deeply? Knowing that Ruthy loved me made me breathe, but knowing how deeply she loved me caused me to question whether I was worthy of the air she breathed. I looked into her eyes, but they asked me questions I simply couldn't answer. I tried, but every time I opened my mouth only silence escaped the gulf between my lips. "How can you love me Ruthy? How can you love a messed up man like me, whose only mission in life has been to be like the monster beneath his mothers sheets? What kind of woman loves a man like that?"
"Pete, when did you find out?"
"What does that have to do with anything? Huh?!"
"Well, the way I see it… The way I see it, it's not like you wanted to be a monster on purpose. Your father did like most of us do, he only showed the good parts, he didn't show you his darkness because he wanted you to walk in the light."

I grew angry at Ruthy's patience shouting in frustration, "What light?! Don't start that Jesus crap with me now. I am trying to tell you that my father was a racist! He was a murderous closet racist! This is the kind of stuff that kids read about in books, this is not my life! And you want to talk to me about light and darkness right now?! What are you going to tell me next, huh? Let me guess, 'Pete you're better than that,' OR 'Pete don't beat yourself up, your father was a good man.' Either way, I don't want to hear it! I want the truth Ruthy," her eyes bulged slightly and she swallowed like she'd been walking across the desert in the heat of the day. "I want you to stop smiling and tell me that you hate my father, tell me you hate me for looking like him. Say something other than 'I understand.' Say... something!"

"Now look, I'm about tired of you taking all of this out on me. I have loved you when no one else did, when your sorry excuse for a father disowned you. Who was there, huh?! Ruthy." Tears streamed down her cheeks and she yelled until veins jumped forward, bouncing from her forehead, neck, and arms. She waved her finger just in front of my nose.

The scent of jasmine, lavender, and ylang ylang invaded my anger. The veins on her hands unlike those I saw on my father and grandfather were beautiful. They coursed with blood that boiled from anger and loss, flowed with grief, and pumped from a heart far stronger than my own. Hearing her voice crack as she blew up for the first time since I'd loved her, I immediately felt guilty for the verbal gasket I'd just blown. She continued and her voice leaped three octaves, "Am I angry?! Absolutely, but you'd better thank God that forgiveness is real, and that I don't let that anger fester into bitterness. I walk in anger, I talk in anger, I breathe in air and breathe out anger...

But you don't get it do you?! Your father hurt me, your grandfather hurt us all. But you, Peter, are only guilty of loving me in every way! I'm angry because you had to choose between me and your family, I'm angry because our children never got to know either grandfather! But that's life Peter. It hurts us, we recover, and we move on! It hurt me, I moved on with you." She said that last piece matter of factly like I should have already known it. I wanted to be upset by her outburst, but I couldn't at all, in fact I was grateful that she let some of these things go. If the truth is to be told, I was grateful because I finally got a piece of the punishment I so desperately thought I deserved.

Had I have known something… Suspected something… Said something… Three powerful men would still be in our lives, but my silence killed them. I was just as much to blame as my father and grandfather, but even Ruthy's piercing words failed to assuage my guilt. I cried… Something broke inside of me and the ravenous droplets within me poured out fiercely. Ruthy's arms took me in and I loved her all the more.

*\* \* \**

*Where pain and healing dwell together*
*There my father is I*
*\* \* \**

# CHAPTER 20

Peter drank almost a full 5th of whiskey on his own. With
each glass he poured, he attempted to drown out the
misery that threatened to overtake him. Sorrows and
failures floated to memory… gulp. They were washed out to sea.
Unrequited love attempted to shake up his calm demeanor, but
another gulp stilled his ship. Disappointments he'd been cursed
to receive and blessed to extend replaying non stop beneath his
blinking eye lids only slowed when he took a swig from a glass
filled with liquid forgiveness. No, he could not ask forgiveness
from those he was aware he had loved unsuccessfully. He mused
inwardly about the possibility of apologizing. But could not bring
himself to do either. His asking forgiveness… apologizing…
Hell, allowing his mind to even think about what had transpired
that night meant admitting his role in things. He wasn't guilty.
He hadn't actually done anything himself. It was them… Sure
he could have spoken up, but what exactly would that have
accomplished?

He had to let those thoughts go, he had to shed this albatross
that continually choked the length of his neck. Each day he
breathed, he inhaled painful remembrance and exhaled sanity. As
guilt crept in, his piece of mind escaped and he was left only with
himself, the empty sound of rattling ice cubes, and clinking

glass. Lost in his morose thoughts, the loud silence interrupted his sadness and he was brought back to reality by the sound of the ice chattering in his cup as he swayed it mindlessly in his raised hand.

No, no… he did not have the option of asking forgiveness. Though he was guilt stricken, he rationalized that he had not actually committed the sin himself. His grandfather was guilty, and his father… his father was a dishonest disgrace to the cloth. But he, the man drowning himself in sips of sorrow saturated with silent contrition… he himself was guilty only of ignorance. The only thing he'd done was stumble upon his fathers secrets. Why then was he riddled with such guilt? Why was he consumed when he knew there was nothing he could have done? There were questions he could not answer, nor could his glass of vodka answer these questions. The warmth his throat felt as each sip poured into his body and set his soul ablaze with numbness was soothing. He was a man on fire, but not in a good way. The heated sensation he felt did answer one question in particular though… What would bring him enough comfort to allow his eyes to close in slumber?

Inhaling deeply, he sucked in the last bits of pain enveloping his being. Slowly he exhaled his anxieties, willing them to stay away. He breathed again, one last time before gulping the remaining liquor from the glass and then from the bottle. With that, he sighed, crossed his arms and allowed his mind to drift lazily asleep. "Jesus," he mumbled. "Jesus," he breathed in His essence and expelled His name in the peace of sleep.

*  *  *

*Where confusion and certainty mix*
*Our souls simultaneously cry*
*  *  *

# CHAPTER 21

Dave and Rich stepped into the front door of our parents home. Ruthy and I were still unsure whether we'd stay in Mississippi or not, so we had cleared most everything from the house. Only our parents favorite chairs, a love seat and a chipped wooden coffee table remained in the living room, and the bed in which Ruthy and I had been sleeping remained in the house. When they stepped in, they exchanged nervous glances… Glances which confirmed my naive suspicion, they had known all these years. Only I had been foolish enough not to know.

They chatted quietly, noticing that the children were still in Hazlehurst with Ruthy's mother, and taking in the rooms vexing emptiness. It, of course was me who broke the silence. "It wasn't in the box in the attic." Dave and Rich exchanged confused glances, then looked at me. As a child I would challenge them with riddles and informal scavenger hunts that were always accompanied by a sleek smile. Today's words were not a riddle, and were not met with a smile. Hearing the gritting of my teeth, I pursed my lips and Dave offered me a face marred with irritation, he always hated word challenges. "What you were looking for… in the attic… while we were cleaning. You remember… Don't you guys?" Suddenly their faces both registered what I was saying with my eyes. "You're wondering how I found it right?

Well first, lets discuss what I found shall we?" I nodded to Ruthy who opened a duffle bag I had stuffed below the coffee table, and shakily laid its contents on the wooden table. "Fellas. Was it the hoods and sheets you were looking for, or was it dad's journal?"

Dumbfounded doesn't exactly describe the look plastered across their faces. More apt words might be awestruck, flabbergasted, guilty, embarrassed, obfuscated. "Is anyone going to say anything, or are you just going to stand there looking… as stupid… as I felt when I made these discoveries?! Huh?!" I was so angry I couldn't control myself. My fists were balled tightly, and my blood pumped so hard, I could feel its redness warming my skin and feeding my frustration with their silence. "Listen Pete, its not what you think." Dave spoke up.

"Oh its not huh? Because what I think is that you knew about Dad's secret and you never bothered to tell me!" Ruthy reached out for my hand, I tried to jerk away. I tugged slightly hoping that my anger would push my feet toward the door. But her love was like quick sand… I sank into it, and when I was afraid and tried to run away, I sank even further. I didn't squeeze back, but I did yield to the firmness of her grip and sat next to her on the love seat. My neck obeyed my legs and bent slightly until my head hung in angst. My eyes lifted slightly and I saw Rich and Dave sit across from us in the only remaining chairs. Having discovered these family secrets I glanced around the room only to discover that my soul felt the way this room looked. Bare, empty… unsatisfied and intoxicated with sadness. Grief poured in with every breath and never escaped. It only filled the empty space where my father's love had once been housed.

"Look Pete, Dave and I didn't hide anything from you. We only found this all out in the past few years. We knew something was going on, but didn't exactly know what was going on. But one Sunday morning, dad asked me to go to the bedroom to get his favorite tie and his suit jacket. I was digging through the closet trying to find the jacket that matched his tie," he eyed me curiously considering whether he should continue. Dave nodded so he did, "when I saw the robes hanging. All the way at the back, behind his black clerical robe. I didn't know what to say… I heard him calling me from downstairs, asking me to hurry with his clothes. We were late for Sunday service, and you know how dad was… As the preacher there was no way he was going to be late to service. After I collected my thoughts, I walked downstairs and confronted him. At first he kept saying crazy things like the devil was in me and that the devil was trying to make him late to service. He even yelled 'get thee behind me Satan!' at me, like that would soothe my emotions. Finally he said it was for the good of our family, snatched the tie out of my hand, and said that whoever was not in the car in the next three minutes would be left. Mom, Dave, and I missed service that Sunday…

When dad got home he was livid and yelling all sorts of things at me. I felt so ashamed and guilty, but I also felt relieved that I finally knew. He yelled until he was exhausted and every time Dave or I opened our mouths to say something he told us that we didn't understand… That life hadn't taught us about sacrifice yet." Realizing that I was partially dismissing the story, Dave spoke up.

"He wouldn't tell us anything Pete. But I was angry and asked if that was the reason he'd hated Libby so much. Dad looked exhausted, like he was speaking French in a room full of Germans. Finally he said, 'you'll never understand until you have to,' and then walked away.

While I had the gumption, I stood up and asked him how in the world he could reconcile being a klansmen with being a Christian. 'I can't, and that's what hurts.' His eyes shifted to mom, to Rich, me and then the carpet. I asked again and he wouldn't reply. Wouldn't say anything... He just walked away and assured us that sooner rather than later we'd know why."

*\* \* \**

*I strolled through life afraid*
*And finally I swallowed my fear*
*\* \* \**

# CHAPTER 22

"I left that night and went to visit Elizabeth, I told her what I had found, and she said that she'd always suspected it. I cried for the first time in a long time, it was like I had lost a part of myself and didn't know if I wanted to search for it. I hated him, and I was so tough on Libby… I took it out on her at first, but she told me she understood my frustration and then she explained something to me that eventually made me see dad in a different light.

She told me that she more than suspected. That actually, she had known, that she had always known, and that most of the blacks in Clarke County either knew or had heard. She added that my father had been good to her and she didn't hate him. I didn't know what to say, why didn't she hate him as much as I did?! She told me to go back home and talk to him, find out why. I hated to admit it, but she was right. That was the night I knew I was in love with her, I mean I'd always loved her… But Pete, suddenly, I understood why," my eyes rested on Ruthy and I abruptly shut my mouth.

It felt good to release all of this; to tell Pete everything I should have told him years ago. Starting with an apology about the way I had treated Ruthy. I could see the disgust in Pete's eyes, and maybe now wasn't the time to offer the apology.

I had been with Elizabeth for years. Everyone had seen the way I'd always looked at her. She was the perfect example of beautiful. Libby had the innocent doe eyes that had seen the worst parts of the world and somehow had gone uncorrupted.

He wanted to be understanding, to listen to what I was telling him about the woman I loved and had been married to for the better part of 20 years. Libby was my heart, my everything… she kept me grounded, and pushed me to grow in Christ. She was the epitome of submission, but not the patriarchal, woman obey your husband definition. Like Ruthy, she submitted biblically. She completely trusted and had faith in her husband's ability and desire to lead her, to love her unconditionally, and to forgive her. She gave her fears and worries to me and desired to please me. Pete wanted to care about our love, and he did… he just couldn't care today. Today he needed his questions answered. Today, he needed to understand why my fathers skin hid beneath crisp white sheets. Today, he was on a mission and my love for Libby was a rabbit trail that he simply was unwilling to explore. Any other day he would have been grateful that the two of us shared the same fulfilling love.

Just not today.

*  *  *

*Through the shards of glass that were myself*
*I finally stared deep into the mirror*
*  *  *

# CHAPTER 23

C uriosity had gotten the best of me, I needed to know who my other siblings were. I understood why my brothers and sisters didn't want to know who they were, but I couldn't understand Dave's insistence that meeting them wasn't a bell that could be un-rung. He seemed to have all of the answers, but knew nothing all at once. Here I was, all over again, trying to piece information together. I didn't care what my family thought, I simply had to know. If I were going to honor my fathers wishes and take over at Sufficient Grace, I needed answers, and I needed them immediately.

I dressed hurriedly, ignoring the blistering stares Dave and Ruthy sent me. On some level I knew that Ruthy understood, she always did. Perhaps she eyed me out of curiosity, and of course there was always the question of how meeting my family might impact my own. The questions plaguing me would have to wait until I got my most burning question answered. I didn't say anything to anyone. I simply put my fathers notebook in the fold of my arm where my chest and biceps met, believing the intersection might cause truth to meet there as well. I hoped that my feet would make the journey in the suns oppressive heat. Stepping out onto the front porch reminded me that such a scorching sun angered even the sweetest of people.

Its furious rays beat my skin until the small amount of melanin I had, rushed to my defense only to accept defeat and slightly darken my pale dermis. Secretly, I relished the moment. My father hated brown people. So much so that he fathered two brown children and abandoned them, withholding the protection a loving father should have afforded his priceless children. I could never leave my babies to the wolves and yet they were the same complexion I imagined my black siblings were... Golden onyx.

I didn't know where to go to find the answers to the questions that I had, and I didn't have anyone who could lead me in the right direction. Dave, being the only one who knew my father's details remained close lipped, trusting that frustration would change my mind. I strolled down the porches stairs, pausing momentarily to inhale the sweet thickness of the Mississippi air. I'd once walked down these very stairs to escape my fathers choking hate, and here I was exploring these same steps some 50 years later to find the children who he'd choked in the very hate I'd once escaped. I mused at the thought that he turned in his grave.

Things looked so different now, the only store in town I recognized was a small co-op. Everything else suggested I had once lived here, but nothing told me what my life had been. Needing to hear from God and ignore my confusion, I walked toward Sufficient Grace Fellowship somehow feeling a magnetic pull back home. The building stood the same, though it's exterior once a bright white with a silver plated steeple was now the color of my abused skin. Light brown.

Poetry couldn't have captured the beauty of the now golden bell that hung just at the zenith of the steeple and swayed in the colorless yet heavy summer wind. Silence sung my name and my feet obeyed the melody. Without realizing it, I'd strolled the quarter mile downtown and was making my way up the steps of Sufficient Grace. It had once been called Righteous Remnant, but that name now belonged to a church just beyond the hanging bridge. When had my father given up the name to his church? And where did he get a name like Sufficient Grace? I stood momentarily encapsulated by outlandish flights of fancy when the church bell rang.

Noon... The hottest hour of the day, in the middle of July, the years hottest month. With sweat beads racing to see which could reach my cotton neckline first, I snapped out of my stupor and reached for the door handle. I was pleased to find the church doors open, but I wasn't ready to walk in. It had been a mere two weeks since my fathers death and I struggled with whether to take over the church; should I even remain in Mississippi? I tucked my questions deep into the pocketed recesses of my mind and shifted my attention to the task at hand. "Lord, I need you now. I trust in you. Amen." Blinking my heavy eyes, I saw for the first time that my answers would come at a price... But thank God Jesus had paid it all.

When I finally stilled myself enough to walk through the door, I stepped in and inhaled the scents of redwood and olive oil. Exhale...No doubt in my mind, I was home. I sat in the last pew on the right. I'd sat there the last two Sundays. Feeling the stained wood rub against my crisp pants suddenly lit a fire in me that being still could not douse. I stood slowly, admiring the craftsmanship with my fingers. We had carved these seats together... My father, my brothers, and I. Once stained the color of red hinted oak, they'd each been sanded, refinished, re-stained and now sparkled red mahogany. I strolled down each aisle humming Amazing Grace. Every time I thought about what a wretch my father was, I got lost in the wood's intricate stories.

I'd never noticed until now that the front row where we used to sit was especially detailed, bearing not only snippets of Amazing Grace, but also people who it appeared might be recipients of that grace.

One held a rope that appeared to lasso only his tears and the other end, a noose, was attached to a heavy cross. Another, a woman carrying a baby, where a larger child from whom she walked, reached out desperately to her. The thickness of the cross held the rope out to her and extended its girth to the child. I was certain that the other carvings told stories as well, but the lyrics of my father's carvings were lost on me.

I wanted to cry, but there were no more tears to shed. Instead, I found myself seated in that row, praying for answers when one more carving caught my eye. A young girl with a ripped skirt being offered a shirt by a man whose ankle was intertwined with the base of the cross. Ruthy and Mr. Asberry? How could my father have known unless he was there. Suddenly, I remembered the familiarity of the voices that night. One had in fact been my father and the other my grandfather. Certainly my memory fooled me. I looked down, flipping through the pages of my father's journal. When I flipped to the last three pages, my jaw dropped. Listed in order by date, victim, and participants were every murder or attack my father had participated in with the Klan. My grandfathers name also appeared, as did the names of others I had once heard were the masked men. I wept openly, and just as I lifted my head I saw a carving on my fathers chair. It was the largest chair on the pulpit as was the case with most head pastors. Vivid images of Ruthy and Zeke's fathers being mutilated, hung, and lit ablaze decorated the width of my fathers chair. Where was the cross in this picture?

Flipping through more of the notebooks pages, I stumbled upon a simple line, "all these years later, I am still seeking forgiveness. This is not a burden I ever desired to bare." I closed the book, now more confused than ever. So transfixed by confusion was I, that I never heard the footsteps coming toward me. He cleared his throat and I jumped to attention only to relax again when I saw the compassion in James eyes. He sat next to me and for a moment said nothing, then, "I see you've come back. What's on your mind?"

*\* \* \**

*And I saw myself un-whole*
*\* \* \**

# CHAPTER 24

These were obviously pieces of my dad that he hadn't wanted anyone to know. How much of this could I trust him with? Certainly James, the assistant pastor my father had trusted with his church could be trusted with his secrets. I looked at him hesitantly, but he didn't flinch. "Where do I start?" My eyes watered, but his demeanor did not change, we sat in silence. "How well did you know my father?" His eyes answered me with solemnity, but his voice clarified. He restated the question, "how well do I know your father?" According to my wife this was a tell tale sign that a man was trying to think up a lie, an excuse, or an escape. Though I hated when she called me on it, I loved that she'd unknowingly given me the heads up. After I said nothing for a while, his eyes pooled momentarily, and the quiver in his bottom lip was almost unnoticeable. Still, I said nothing. I wanted to hear the truth but did not want to prompt his confession in any way. Exhaling suddenly, James asked, "what exactly did you want to know?"

Instead of answering his question I made sure that no one was around to hear and then told him everything. I explained that my father who we'd just buried had been a klan member for years, that he'd left things to two African American children we never knew he had, and finally I told him about the notebook and sheets I'd found in his home.

When I finished I felt relieved. I felt like I'd been carrying a weight on my shoulders that only confession could release. For the first time when telling this truth, I didn't cry and my voice didn't waver. My breathing slowed and felt more like a reward and less like the labor it had been. James said nothing. I waited patiently, and just as I felt like he was studying me with his eyes I opened my mouth in frustration. Two minutes of silence was like asphyxiation and my concern for his opinion was birthed. Just as I cleared my throat to speak, he interrupted. "Give me a minute," he held his hand up though his head hung in the same way that Ruthy's did. I stared at his index finger, then at his entire hand. James was about my age, and I noticed that his hands were large and soiled the way my fathers had always been. No wonder they worked together so closely.

I could tell that James was a bit taken aback by my question, but I couldn't quite understand why. Finally he spoke, "I never thought we'd meet this way." His statement was so full of certainty that I had to work overtime to follow along. I remained silent, hoping that my head would have a chance to catch up with my mouth. "By the look on your face I can see that Dad didn't tell you the reason why he wanted you to take over here at Sufficient Grace." My mind swirled, did he just say Dad? I was certain he would tell me who his father was, but the words that followed took my breath away. "He wanted you to take over so that you could work alongside your younger brother." I can't say what I was thinking, feeling, or saying. At that moment I seemed to merely be existing. Brother? There was absolutely no way that James could be my brother, except... There were those hands, large and worn like my fathers. There were these hazel eyes with dashes of aqua that drowned my sorrow and kept my joy afloat. Could this be true?

Like Ruthy, James saw beyond my firm jawline and heard the questions that only my eyes could ask. "You're probably trying to put this all together, so I suppose I should explain what I can." "Can I hug you?" I mumbled hoping that my lips had uttered what my heart whispered. I had found the brother I'd never known I had, a hug would officially bring us together. Gifting me with a nod and a sigh of relief, we embraced for the first time and I felt like we'd never been apart. Anger rose in me because my father had deprived us of his whole self, and of each other.

"I'll start with this," James began earnestly. "I always knew who dad was, and for years I hated him... I hated him for loving my mother, I hated him for not loving us, and I hated him because he loved you guys. I couldn't understand a man who could have two families... A man who I'd always known was my father, but who I was never allowed to address in public without lowering my eyes and treating him like every other white man. I can't even say that hate describes the way I felt about him. But, one day he had this change of heart. It was a Sunday night. He came by the house upset about something, and told my mother that he was tired of hiding. He apologized for the first time and he wept the way I imagined Jesus did when he discovered that his friend Lazarus died. He said that he'd always struggled with the way he'd treated us and my mother.
That he felt guilty for his life and that he owed us his love, perhaps more. I was so angry Pete, I could see through his tears... I could see through his guilt, and I could see through his pain. I saw a monster. I saw a man who didn't know who he was and didn't love himself enough to love his seed. I saw my father and it terrified me that I might be just like him. My fear made me more angry at him, and then I was angry at myself for ever wanting to be like him, for ever wanting to know him. I was enraged and

angry and hurt, and all these other things that I could never quite put my finger on. I couldn't even name the hurt that held me on the day he came by, so I let it fester into more anger, and I held onto that anger because it was comfortable... It was who I was, it had taken me over."

As James carried on, I could see that his emotions truly stung. He seemed dazed; stuck in the past almost, and trapped between being who he once was and simply remembering. I felt sorry for him, but listening to his rambling gave me sorrow for my own self too. On that day as we sorrowed together, I let him be transparent, and I saw dejection in a way I'd never been privy to before. In him I saw my father, and through that I saw myself. I gazed at the beautiful stained glass windows and asked simply, "how did you get past it all? Why aren't you angry now?"

His reply. "I am angry. I just don't let the anger control me... Besides, the more I thought about his guilt and his sin the more I realized, I had to be forgiven of my sins too, I was just blessed enough that only God knew what my sins were."

Pausing for me to chew a moment, he continued, "dad could see my venom and he could see wrath in my eyes. I needed him to explain but I was too angry to ask. I just seethed quietly as he spoke. Finally, he spoke to me and the more he explained, the more I understood. I hated him for it and I hated the truth, but I needed to know it and I couldn't heal without it. In the long run, realizing that God is truly in the business of changing people, me included, made way for me to forgive and to join him in his ministry. Dad really was a good man."

God must have done some serious moving in James life. I couldn't get past secrets and forgive my dead father, yet he had lived through my father's worst moments and still managed to.

I had some repenting to do and somewhere inside I knew there was no forgiveness for me if I gave no forgiveness to him. My heart was hardened in a way I'd never felt before, but the more James told me, the more I could feel my steel resolve melting away. "So what exactly did he tell you that made you understand so much? I need to hear it... Everything, because I'm struggling right now. I'm feeling the same way you felt."

James looked to me briefly as if he was looking through me to see if I was actually ready. "I can see how this is all weighing you down. You look exhausted. Are you sure you want to know this?" I was too exhausted to be offended. I exhaled heavily, and answered his question with a lengthy blink and a silent nod. Silence blasted my thoughts and I looked up to meet his eyes. He began hesitantly.

*  *  *

*I saw the joy that had once been there*
*Joy my bitterness stole*

*  *  *

# CHAPTER 25

I n all honesty, I was excited about Pete going to meet his brother and sister. I had no idea where he was going to start searching, but I trusted that God would lead him in the right direction if he could just calm himself enough to be led. I hated to see my husband in this way, but I knew that he needed to go through it. And as much as it hurt to watch, he needed to go it alone. I couldn't carry him through his pain and I couldn't lead him to a place of peace. That had to be done by the Holy Spirit, and my interference would just disrupt his process. I feared whether he was ready for the truth he was walking into, but somehow I knew that God would not leave him alone and broken in His midst.

Sitting in the comfort of Pete's parents home, I searched for things to say to Dave, but the only thing that came out was silence intermingled with moist air. Finally Dave spoke up, "Pete isn't ready to know about my father. I mean, he had a heart attack the last time he asked a question, and knowing the rest is certain to kill him." His eyes were wet with worry, but I felt no pity for him. He knew more than he was telling and I wanted to know every stabbing detail. "Enlighten me Dave. This family has had too many secrets for too long, so... Do me a favor and fill me in." Dave looked surprised at my bluntness, but obliged me.

"That Sunday when I found out, dad took off and stayed gone for 2or 3 days. No one knew where he went, but mom. She seemed to know something the rest of us were missing. She'd heard rumors about a black woman he was messing around with. When he came home Tuesday, he looked relieved, but the moment he saw my face worry struck him. He said nothing at first and went to his room, got a duffel bag and began filling it. It was early in the evening so the sun hadn't set yet. Still, it felt like it was well into the night when he came out and announced that he was leaving. Mom told me to leave so they could talk, which I did. I went to Elizabeth's where I stayed until darkness cloaked the sky. I had no business being there so late at night, but we sat on the porch, longing to express the compassion we each had but could not show because our skin was mismatched.

I enjoyed the tension, it made me love her more... But the more I sat, the more I had this odd feeling that I needed to go back to the house. It was a horribly nagging feeling, and I prayed and sat in silence, but the feeling grew stronger. Eventually, around 10 that night, I got in my truck and came back here to see my mom and dad.

When I pulled up, I just saw smoke and flames. I couldn't grasp what was going on, but I could see mom screaming frantically, 'he's still in there, someone help!' There were firefighters sitting in their trucks, watching the flames lick the sky and caress the curve of the antebellum ceilings, but they never moved. When I neared my mother she was still screaming, but this time at them, 'aren't you going to help? You're just gonna let him die?! If you're not gonna help him, you should just leave... I wish you were in the fire too!' Some laughed, others appeared to be convicted by their inaction."

I didn't understand what exactly Dave was telling me. How, in such a short span of time had the house caught fire, and why was Pete Sr. the only person still inside? For every leaping flame, a family of questions danced through my head.

"Mother was screaming and crying. I was dumbfounded, but the heat from the flames melted any helplessness that I might have felt. When I realized these men were just going to let dad die, I grabbed the water hose and sprayed as much as it would let me. Nothing seemed to soften the despair of the flames, and my futile attempts to calm them only seemed to ignite their fury. Neighbors strolled over carelessly with buckets, and hoses, some feigning helpful attempts and others struggling to kill the heats intense breaths.

"Still, the fire seemed to be screaming obscenities... Laughing at us trying to extinguish it. Through all the confusion, I realized that mom was still screaming, and dad had not come out. I went to the back door where there was only smoke lingering, no flames yet. I could hear noises so I went inside to find him, and could hear faint coughing sounds. His coughs were getting increasingly weak until I couldn't hear him anymore. I was calling out to him, asking for any sign that he was still alive. But other than the sounds coming from outside, the pounding heartbeats I felt, and the fire popping I heard nothing. Ruthy, I almost gave up... My eyes were burning from the smoke and I couldn't see anything, I was starting to choke."

Dave cried silently as he recounted the story. It was almost as if he was reliving it all over again. This must have been why their father loved Dave so much, and said in his letter that he *owed* Dave so much.

"Somehow I made it all the way through the back porch and into the kitchen doorway. I had my eyes closed, but I tried to feel my way around so I could find him. After what felt like forever I couldn't find him, hear him, and even when I blinked a little I couldn't see him. I turned to run out and boom," he clapped his hands to illustrate, "I ran into the kitchen table. I was in serious pain and tried to lean up against one of the chairs to steady myself, but when I reached over I felt my fathers shoulders. I hoisted him out of the chair and dragged him from the house just as the flames reached into the kitchen and snatched away it's tranquility. When I came around the side of the house dragging him, my mother ran over and helped me lift his legs. We struggled, but between the two of us, we carried him to the trucks flatbed and placed him in. I drove like a banshee all the way to the Hospital. When dad came to, he was groggy and seemed upset that I'd saved him. The first thing he said was, 'you shoulda just let em' kill me.' I didn't ask too many questions, just let him mumble until he fell asleep."

*  *  *

*I saw me walking, wounded and weak*

*  *  *

# CHAPTER 26

"They wouldn't let us see him. A black family in a white hospital, visiting a reputable white man. It was simply unheard of. I didn't know if the klan had set his house on fire because of us, because he was finally walking away from them, or because they knew that his influence could've brought people together all over down here. Mom and I were confused, but we waited until her next shift cooking at the hospital so that we could get whatever news was available." No matter how I felt, or what kind of reaction I had, James never stopped telling the story. I was so captivated by the details that I almost lost my breath at points. So many pieces to a puzzle I'd been vehemently trying to leave in shambles were being placed before me. Maybe my father actually had a heart, and I, like him, needed to reexamine mine. When James drew a deep breath I interrupted, "so... Your mother was a cook?"

"Is. Her name is Tamar, and yes she's still living, but she was a cook then. There were few jobs a woman could have back then, and even fewer jobs that a black woman could have. Mother, maid, nanny, or cook... For her, the least degrading job was cooking, and she was supporting us alone, so she cooked for people who hated her but loved her food. I'll never quite understand it. Her food was a reflection of her, and white people loved it... Her femininity was her, and a white man loved it... But it seemed they looked beyond her humanness, ignoring it almost, and saw only what they thought she had to offer. No white person, even our father ever came to know her fullness because of that."

"Wow, how could she fall in love with a man like that?" I asked not understanding that I'd neglected to know Ruthy fully as well; seeing her strength and support as something merely to be used and admired, not as something to be understood. I cherished her, but perhaps I'd not given her the gift of knowing her beyond the unconditional love she'd given me. I had wanted to be like my father all these years... I guess I'd gotten my wish.

James lowered his eyes this time, "I don't think she was in love at first. When a white man told you to do something you did it. Questioning could get you hurt, killed, or get those close to you killed. When dad showed interest, she was required to tell him yes, that's just what it was. It was the law and there was nothing she could do about it. But the more he showed up to see her, the more of himself he showed her, and she came to look forward to seeing him. He saw her as a person, though he couldn't see everything in her, he did see her. That's what she grew to love. No one said much to her... Black people either thought she was acting like she was better than them because she had a white man, saw her as a fool for loving a man whose father was so hateful, or hated her because their humanity had never been seen. It was rough; but we made it through."

James eyes rolled toward the ceiling as he searched for his next batch of words. I didn't know what to say, but I was burning to ask, "how do you know it was that klan that set the house on fire?" His reply slapped me back to the reality I'd once lived in.

"Well. First, do you remember I told you that dad came by the house? He stayed there until Tuesday afternoon. Monday night, a rock came through the front window. It said that he better pick the right sheets or we were all dead. My mom was terrified, and dad told us to pack. That Tuesday he'd take us somewhere safe. I went to the room my sister and I shared, and began to pack our clothes. She saw this bright light and a bunch of what she called ghosts running from the light. I went to the window and looked out, and there was a cross burning on the lawn.

We couldn't even scream because we were so afraid. It took me a few minutes to digest everything that was happening, but after a moment or two I grabbed my sisters hand and pulled her to the front room where mom and dad were. It was almost like... they could see the terror in our eyes, I don't know that anyone knew what to say. The only place to run was outside, so we huddled together praying that the only thing to be lynched that night was a wooden sign of redemption. Dad felt responsible, he planned to go home late that evening but with the rock... And the cross... He couldn't leave us like that. He said he'd subjected us to enough torment, he didn't want to leave us unprotected anymore.

We thought our lives were in danger, but the reality was that his love for us put his life in danger. For the klan, it was one thing to rape a black woman, or have a little thing on the side. But to love her; to be loyal to her; to protect her in anyway, that was a move that could get you killed. It was like blaspheming their doctrine of hate. Love just doesn't go along with it."

James tilted his head as if he were trying to answer questions about the behavior of light in a vacuum on Venus. After a brief moment he spoke up like his words stole the very life from his soul, "it's ironic. Serving a God who is love, and so ferociously hating the very people he'd belong to if he were living today... Our darkness made us a peculiar people, misunderstood by everyone, at times even by our own selves. The epistles perfectly sum up the law as loving your neighbor. It never defines neighbor, except to say that all who were formed by the creator are your neighbor.

All these years later, I still can't understand why it was so impossible for us to be loved. White sheets blinded those men from realizing that we all came from the same God. But dad, he got it. He may not have done it right, but I had to forgive him Peter. I had to forgive him, because the God I love has forgiven me for my anger and my hate, and all else that I've done. All these years later, the anger never escapes me, but I forgive those sheeted men and I love them enough to pray for their salvation."

With tears in his eyes that journeyed down his cheeks along the train tracks between joy and pain, he said something that pierced me to my core. "Dad's evil was a blessing. His change, and my families forgiveness... It brought three of those men here to this church, and after some time, they've come to accept me and to know me and love me.

This is a Black congregation. The only whites here are the few men that used to hide under hoods and sheets, and you if you'll stay." I had more questions still, but for now the best I could do was remain with my brother this bitter hour, and mourn the loss of love we both missed in our dad. I'd walked into this church angry, confused, and in desperate need of peace. When I returned home to my wife, Dave, and Rich; I did it full of peace, forgiveness, and with more understanding than I'd had since I left Mississippi so many years ago.

*  *  *

*I had no strength or power*
*And here, I thought I was meek*
*  *  *

# CHAPTER 27

D ave had filled in nearly all of my blanks. I now knew why the house though familiar had been different than I'd remembered. Pete and I had not even known there was a second fire. It made me wonder if the fire that first caught Peters house just after my fathers death was because of the klan too. I was prepared to ask Dave, but before I could, Peter came through the door. "I met my other brother. He's the assistant pastor, at the church. He told me a lot, and Dave I get it..." Dave exhaled suddenly like he'd been holding his breath since his birth. Peter and Dave were silent, but their eyes pierced the thickness of the afternoon air. For once though, it was a pleasant thickness, unlike what had been choking us since we'd arrived just a few week ago.

"I invited them to dinner. James and Martha both, and their mother Tamar. Ruthy call your mother. Dave, Rich you call the others. We need to be together for once. Tonight, we'll eat together, lay it all out on the table... This may be our last opportunity to do what should have happened years ago. I want everyone here at 7." Dave, Rich, and I exchanged hurried glances. Peter was calm, too calm almost. Usually, I could read my husband like a book, but it was as if he'd been rewritten by Shakespeare and I couldn't follow his lead. I had three hours to

But I had to take a moment to pray, to collect my thoughts, to prepare my heart for whatever would unfold at the table. I said what Dave and Rich were thinking, "Pete, are you sure you wanna do that? It's a lot for your heart to take. Having them in the same room as Jane and Earl might not be such a good idea. I was thinking-" Holding up his hand, Peter halted my words. "They need to be invited. They don't have to like it, they don't have to show up, but the Lord works in mysterious ways, and we'll just let him do his work. This is a family dinner... They are family." "Pete, we'll call everybody, I hope you're sure about this." Rich spoke up, "but I won't tell them about James and Martha. If I do-" "We won't trick them, or lie to them. That's how we ended up in this situation..." Something about Pete's resolve was comforting to us all. Somewhere in coming to know himself, his father, and his truth... Peter had a peace that none of us could understand.

But, there again was the power of God. In the midst of an emotional tsunami, Pete seemed to be strolling above the superficial flow of waters that sought his life. But still there was peace in the storm, and he'd managed to procure wisdom in this confusion.

*  *  *

*Pieces of myself dripping with hurt*
*Floated through a lake of fire blazing sin*

*  *  *

# CHAPTER 28

"You guys did call everybody right?" As always; Rich, Dave, and Ruthy glared at me and then looked at each other. When no one replied I said, "Well… did you?" This time Rich answered, "I did." I stared at him blankly, awaiting further explanation, but nothing came. "I didn't hear anything from Earl, but Suzy said she wasn't coming. Didn't want to be around any N-" Jane stopped short of insulting us all. "Well, you know what I'm saying." She smirked as she made momentary contact with every set of brown eyes in the room and then locked eyes with Ruthy. I thought to speak up in order to alleviate the tension but decided against it. Without leaving her gaze, Ruthy spoke up, "That's a shame. Let's make sure we put enough aside for the both of them. Shall we pray?" "I was thinking the same thing," James interjected. "They shouldn't have to miss out just because they couldn't make it, and neither should we." Ruthy nodded, pleased with her response, and no doubt wondering why she was married to a man whose hateful family history kept making appearances in her life.

Silent tautness filled the gaping holes between our lips so much so that there was no room for words. Ruthy did what none of the rest of us could do, "James would you like to pray?" I agreed, and then turned to James just in time to notice Earls entrance.

"Good to see you brother. I saved a seat for you right here, next to me." Surprised by James' invitation, Earl sat slowly in the flawlessly stained chair. Earl appeared uneasy, but I was pleased that he obliged James and kept his remaining thoughts to himself. Having prayed and dished plates out for the children who we sat at a nearby table, we silently tore into the feast before us.

Covering the length of the table was fried pork chops, fried chicken, lima beans and baked chicken. The available spaces were occupied by corned bread, potato salad, Caesar salad, green beans, macaroni and cheese, and at least five other dishes. Cakes, pies and other sweets littered the kitchen counter tops and their scents mingled with the aroma of stale hatred and excited salivation. Ruthy had outdone herself this time. With Elizabeth's help, there was absolutely no way anyone could deny themselves of the perfection upon which their eyes rested, and their nostrils happily opened themselves to.

***

*I looked good on the outside*
*But my mess was within*
***

# CHAPTER 29

Jane had warned me not to come, but I had to see it for myself. There was no way one of those monkeys was going to out dress me, so I put on my clean khaki pants and a freshly washed button down shirt. My shirt was crisp and white, just like the skin I was born in. I came only a few minutes late, and not only had they started without me but they had let that filthy thing at the table pray. Did he really think God was listening to his prayer? His skin was its color because of God cursing Ham, if God cursed him why would his prayer be honored?

After hearing the pastor preach last Sunday out of Colossians 3 and 1Timothy 5 about the necessity of family, I thought maybe I should pop in and grace them with my presence. I'd been standing in the doorway long enough to be sick to my stomach. I was nice enough to let him say Amen before I offered a prayer that God would actually hear. Just as I was getting to the good part, Rich shouted Amen! I let him have his little victory, and even sat by the bastard James. I would always hate him. Granted, the only thing he had done to deserve my hatred was be born a Black man; but as far as I was concerned his birth was more than enough.

Thankfully though there was enough food in front of me to keep us both busy. He was so busy chomping that he said little to me, and I was so busy salivating I pretended momentarily that he didn't exist. My eyes were probably a little too big for my head because I piled spoon-fulls of everything on my plate! I hated that my brothers had attached themselves to these brown heathens, but today was a special day.

Today I hated everyone at the table equally. I hated the brown ones becuase the sun showered them with additional love and kissed their skin in a way it had never kissed mine. And the white ones, I hated them because they couldn't understand my anger and embarrassment. How could I love any of them? There was an unexplainable part of me that hated myself, so certainly I had no room to genuinely love any of them. It was simply impossible for me to open up my eyes to see their humanness or my heart to love their wholeness.

*  *  *

*I became my father*
*I was unaware and now free to go*
*  *  *

# CHAPTER 30

I had taught my children all these great things about being immaculate people. But not only was I keeping a secret that pulled the life from my chest with each daily reminder, there was one person I had neglected to teach them about. Sitting at this table broke my heart into infinite pieces. Never before had I been in the presence of so many people who had been harmed by a man who in all of his sin had only tried to shield them from the wrath that breathed from the old wooden pulpit every Sunday morning, and then met up with evil in the midnight backwoods to commit the very sins he condemned. Never before had I been unable to shield my eyes even for a moment from the cloud of darkness that threatened to squeeze the rain from my dipped hazel eyes.

I enjoyed the façade of peace that captured my polar family. "Earl, Jane, it's been years since I've seen the two of you. How have you been?" Earl stared at me blankly, like a ghost had spoken to him. It was Jane's eyes though that pierced me to my core. She stared at me as if she knew my soul bore the secret that would set hers free. Responses were trapped deep in their throats, words that my own hoped to set free. Silence. Almost a full minute after my question left my lips, I regretted its departure. My attempt to slice through the dense disdain that filled the room was meritless.

I willed them to speak, but they rejected my advances and returned my request with a chorus of piercing glances. Finally, I cast my eyes down and joined in with the symphony of chewing when I gathered a sinfully large forkful of macaroni and cheese on my plate. My favorite. Earl's favorite too. Jane, who I'd missed all these years, and Suzie... My dear Suzie. Earl and Jane followed suit enjoying the dish, which I'd prepared because I knew they loved it. Suzie had not even allowed us her presence. The children who had once suckled my breast, knew not of their grandfathers silent sins. They knew only how much they loved my macaroni and cheese.

Occasionally, there was small talk between us all. Just when the roaring of plentiful banter would reach the deepest parts of the ear, Earl would clear his throat and grunt. He was just like his father, and I hated him for that, but only I knew why. Only I knew the root of that hate, and only I knew who his father was. That secret ate away at me. It was information I'd hidden for over 30 years. Information I had intended to take to my grave. "Secrets out, we all know what kind of man daddy was. So why are you guys here?

Jane spoke up out of nowhere. I hadn't expected her bluntness, especially because she hadn't the whole truth. Without thinking, I retorted, "your father wasn't the man you think he was."

"And what is that supposed to mean?" This time the bluntness of Jane's tongue didn't surprise me. Her straightforward nature mirrored my own. But, it wasn't like mine; it was mine. She'd inherited it from me, and she'd never know it if I could help it. For a moment I said nothing outwardly. Instead I looked into her eyes and silently asked God to reveal what my lips could not. "It just means that there is a lot you don't know about your family. My skin is not the darkest secret your family has."

With that, Jane placed a fork full of my macaroni and cheese into her mouth. She chewed it completely, never breaking my gaze. When she speared a helping of greens into her mouth, she shrugged her shoulders and turned away from me. As much as my flesh wanted to un-turn every family stone, the Holy Spirit comforted me.

It seemed the silence that proceeded our exchange was as loud as the struggle within my soul. I couldn't take the noise, so I excused myself to the bathroom. I sat on the closed toilet and rested my face in my hands. What was I supposed to do? Each sound that escaped my body threatened to expose my secrets and my shame. These grown children needed to know the truth. They had no idea who they were, or for that matter, what they were. After splashing cool water against my face, I glanced in the mirror and traced the creases of my brown skin. Coffee was the best way I could describe my color. Somehow the very color of the drink that woke people up and gave them life had become the butt of too many jokes.

Tar baby was probably the one that hurt the most. It was the name I'd been called when I was raped by the great white hype, my cousin... Pete's Grandfather, Amnon Thomas. Not like I was the first one he'd violated and I certainly wasn't the last. I was the first though, to bare him children. How could I possibly tell these children the truth after so many years? I couldn't... I wouldn't... But they needed to know. Having felt the coolness of the water and traced the folds of my skin, I returned to the dining room only to lay eyes on my baby girl. There sat Suzie, looking as uncomfortable as she always had. What I knew, could not remain secret. My days were short, and while I'd sworn to take the secret to the grave, its gatekeepers were gone and I no longer felt bound.

Tears pooled in my eyes and staring at her bitter beauty caused me to lose my balance. The smirk that splashed across her face was the pinnacle of bitter sweet for me. "Suzie, I-" before I could finish Esther, Ruthy's mother stood, helped me to stand straight then walked me onto the back porch. "What are you doing?! You can't tell them everything. Not today! Not like this!" She whispered forcefully, like she was afraid raising her voice would hurt me.

"When?! If not now, when? Its beeen more than 30 years, and none of them know." In that moment, all of the anger I'd suppressed was bubbling to the surface. Each exhale released my shame, my secrets, and my hurt. Hell bent on telling the truth, I quickly did an aboutface only to meet the eyes of James and Pete. They only wanted to know that I was alright. I did my best to convince them that I was fine and merely suffering from excitement. Esther said little but somehow convinced them to let me go sit back at the table. Barely steadied and rushing out, Pete's voice penetrated my very being. "What did you mean when you said that my dad wasn't who we thought he was?"
"Pete, please. Let's not do this now." I had never been happier to hear the sound of Esther's voice. Lead weighted my feet down and a hefty cat laid claim on my tongue. "Enough secrets. James and I need to know. What did you mean?" How was I supposed to answer? I responded quickly, "Oh, I was talking to Jane honey."
"Mom," James took my hand and destroyed my will power with the peace I felt in his gaze. "We need to know." Exhale. I hoped that God would forgive me for breaking my vow. I looked at Esther, and she nodded her head for me to begin.

With reservation, I did.

* * *

*I became my father*
*And I finally know who $I$ is*

* * *

# CHAPTER 31

I was unprepared for what she had to say. As far as I knew, we never kept secrets from each other. But this was no ordinary secret, and as much as the truth stabbed me deep in the chest, I had to allow my heart to take in what my mind could not. Peter seemed to be struggling just as much as I. Maybe even more. The trees of manhood that had been his father and grandfather were chopped down in a matter of seconds.

Her story began, no different than what I had read in history books and heard from so many. "Peter, your father and I had… Guys, your dad and I grew up together. My granny was their maid and the family was nice enough to let her bring us around some days. I realize now there were reasons why, but no one ever spoke of it. When you asked certain questions, grown folk would light you up for meddling." Though she was finally letting the cat out of the bag, something deep inside of me knew there was more to be told.

Holding on to my questions, I stared in disbelief at the tale woven by my mother. I hated to see her so uncomfortable, but I had to know. So silent I remained, and patiently my brother and I anticipated each curve and bend of the story.

* * *

*I became my faither*
*And I found God in my pieces*

* * *

# CHAPTER 32

I'd never told this story to anyone. My mother knew, but anyone with a brain could've figured it out. I just hoped the boys wouldn't make me spell things out in too much detail. God help me, I just wasn't sure I could bare my soul in this way. "We had always been nice to each other, but we loved each other. I can't say when exactly I knew I loved him, nor do I know when he realized he loved me. But he did.

Your father was angry that he couldn't invite me to the big end of the year dance, so he chose not to go at all. The night of the dance, his parents went out to dinner, and well, I almost broke the vow I'd made to God. But your father told me that we would make things right when we got married. I knew that Amnon, his father would never agree to us marrying. Amnon was the grand marshal of the Mississippi White Knights of the Klu Klux Klan, and his mother… Well let's just say that she was a very gentle version of Amnon. Everyone knew how she felt about Blacks, and her words could slice you open though her smile never faded. You can imagine how angry they both were when they came home from dinner that night only to find me adjusting my wrinkled blouse." It seemed that I was the only person feeling uncomfortable when I spoke about sex, so I continued my story quickly, before I was filled with cowardice.

"I hurriedly ran out of the room, but I could hear Amnon screaming violently. In the midst of the yelling and Pete Sr. trying to dodge his mother's fists and words, the last thing I heard was Amnon's voice. 'It never hurts to have a little coon on the side, but that's all they're good for... the side.' To him, I was a coon... an animal to be haunted; a scavenger, eaten by humans who exercised power over it. I was so much less than human to them. So I ran home, to Big Momma. She didn't ask me any questions, but she was a smart woman, she knew. I cried until I fell asleep."

Before I could move on to the next part of the story I felt anxiety creeping in. Tears eased from the creases of my eyes and hindered every bit of courage that allowed words to flow from my lips. Hoping to maintain my composure, I squeezed my eyes and wished for each uninvited breath to slow and submit to my desire for peace within.

The more I hoped for my personal calamity to turn to calm, the more desperate my search for air became. Hyperventilating, I allowed Esther's arms to gently lower me to the porches single chair. When I found my breath, I found my calm, my courage, and my peace. Now feeling compelled to break the secret chains I had been forced to carry, I put my shame and embarrassment aside. "Almost a week later, I still hadn't spoken to Pete Sr. I hoped that by then everyone would have just forgotten about me getting caught at the house, but... It was Friday afternoon when I finally saw him again. I remember, I was walking downtown just outside of the bank when a white woman walked toward me.

I knew not to look her in the eye, so I cast my eyes on the sidewalk. I stepped down off the curb, but I guess I didn't step down far enough. I can't say exactly, but the next thing I know I felt this hand glide across my face, then there were a fury of feet hitting me everywhere. I couldn't even scream because of the flying dust and gravel.

There was laughter and screaming. Then suddenly it all stopped. When the blows disappeared and the dust settled enough for me to see the sky, I stood as quickly as possible. Holding my ribs and ignoring the pain shooting from my head to each of my toes, I scrambled away from them all. As I started along the sidewalk, I saw Pete Sr. and your grandfather. They'd watched the entire thing.

With a smirk, I heard your grandfather tell Pete Sr., 'told you about those spooks. They just can't keep their clothes on.' It was only then that I looked down and saw scraps of what used to be my shirt freely revealing what God had given me. My left leg was bleeding, and my socks and shoes were filthy. I continued home, but not before I went to her house," I motioned to Esther. "She gave me fresh clothes and cleaned me up. I took the long painful 3 mile walk the rest of the way home from school. The whole walk home I kept replaying the scene in my head. It was like something from a movie. I knew it happened to people, but it didn't happen to me.

Why me?"

Here I was, more than 50 years later and I could still smell the palms of Magnolia trees and envision the red clay that covered my ruined patent leather shoes. I had never told this story before today, but I had relieved it more times than I could count. I hadn't realized it, but tears began to stream down my face as I disclosed what was perhaps the worst moment of my life.

"I was so busy trying to figure out what had just happened to me that I never heard the footsteps or the trucks engine shut off. I smelled something rancid but I thought that maybe the hovering crows were there because a dead animal lay in the bush. I was so stupid not to know it was coming. It wasn't until I was jerked into a small gathering of trees and the fear stealing my scream whispered to me that the crow hovered because it knew something I did not. Some part of me would die in that gathering, and I could never revive that part of myself. Your grandfather, Amnon, he… I felt him prying my legs open, and the more I kicked and clawed, the more he laughed and tugged. I felt him rip away the last bits of my urine stained panties, and turned away just in time to see my innocence running for dear life. A stabbing pain pierced my insides, and I watched her crash to the ground; I reached out for her. I hit him in the head, hoping to get up from the grass and over to my innocence. I lurched forward just in time for a heavy tree branch to make its mark across my face and all I saw was black. I could hear him, I could smell him, I could feel great pain. But my world remained black for some time. When he removed his weight from my body, I was suddenly aware that I had not been breathing. Inhaling deeply and blinking profusely, my vision slowly returned. He zipped his pants, and threw down the stick he'd used to rip my insides apart. He spat in my face, and when I reached forward to wipe it away he said, "you're an Ape, always have been and always will be. Every time you breathe in my son's direction I will remind you of what apes deserve. Use that spit to clean yourself up." With that, he strolled away.

I stood, to run the rest of the way home, but what I saw broke me more than the attacks ever could. There sat Pete Sr., on the bed of the truck, not even 5 yards away. Holding his arms was the burly sheriff and another man held his face. He'd been forced to watch the entire thing. I saw him crying helplessly. I stood naked, ashamed, and radiating with pain. My shame did not come from the attack, I was not responsible for that. I hated Amnon for what he'd done, and I hated your father.

Not only was he powerless to help, but he'd discovered my nakedness for the first time on that day.

I became just the same as every other girl I'd grown up with. Victim to people so powerless they couldn't exist unless they took mine. I left school for a year and went to work with my granny. I washed clothes for Amnon. He was your grandfather, and the man who'd murdered my innocence and then took from me the only good thing to come of it.

By this time, Pete Sr. had married a nice white woman, Leah. Shortly after their marriage, I gave birth to the most gorgeous baby girl, but Amnon took her from me and gave her to Leah and Pete Sr. to raise. They named her Jane and your mother raised her as her own. I worked as the nanny, so even though I couldn't raise my baby, I was able to take care of her. Jane, like your grandfather had blue eyes and sandy hair. She didn't look anything like me, so no one ever knew that she was my child."

I worked as the nanny, so even though I couldn't raise my baby I was able to take care of her. Jane, like your grandfather had blue eyes and sandy hair, she didn't look anything like me, so no one ever knew that she was my child."

"My grandfather was a better man than that! And if he raped you, you deserved it." Somehow Suzie had made it onto the porch and heard what I was finally confessing. "Suzie, there is so much you don't know. Please, you've got to believe me. You need to know." I searched her eyes for even a hint of what she had to feel. Compassion? A connection? The moment I thought I discovered gentleness in her she called for the others to join us. When everyone came outside, I knew there was no turning back.

"Leah loved Pete Sr. beyond life. You would have thought that I'd just walk away from everything, but Leah and I weren't all that different.

As much as I hated Pete Sr., I loved him with every fiber of my being. It might have been wrong, but even still we eventually became intimate. Leah and I were pregnant at the same time, I glanced at Martha and then at Rich. They were only months apart. Almost exactly a year after you two were born, Leah gave birth to Dave. Three years later I got pregnant with Suzie, then almost a year later Leah found out she was pregnant with Pete."

At times the story was even a lot for me to swallow. When Amnon raped me, I got pregnant with Jane and that bastard had taken my daughter away from me. I can only imagine how Leah felt having to raise my child.

If only I had been strong enough to stay away from Pete Sr., I might have never given birth to Martha and Suzie. The only reason I was able to raise Martha, was because she looked like me. It was obvious that she was Black and I guess her skin had been a blessing, because I was able to keep my baby as raise her as my own.

Having taken a deep breath, I lowered a bomb that no one was prepared for… "When your grandfather realized that your father and I were not only involved, but had two children together, he convinced Leah that I'd been stealing from her and had me fired. Amnon made me leave Suzie there with Leah and Pete Sr. I regretted leaving her, but I had no choice. I regretted leaving all of you, but Amnon threatened to hurt you, and since you were light enough to pass I did as he requested. You just didn't tell a White man no back then… And I was terrified of what might happen if I did. Besides, Leah never mistreated any of you, so I knew you would be well taken care of.

The distance didn't stop the love I felt for your father, but it did slow down the time we had together.More than three months went by and we hadn't spoken. I missed Pete Sr. but I knew that eventually we'd be together again. One night I was home with Martha when I heard dogs barking. I stepped out back to see what it was, and when I came back in Amnon was standing there. I tried to run, but his hate was strong and so were his arms. I lost another crucial part of myself that night, my joy.

This time, I had twins. Amnon took one of them, the one with blue eyes and dropped him off with Pete Sr. and Leah. I never told anyone, until now."

Earl demanded to know who the twins were. We all stared at him until he realized, that he was the twin. He shouted at no one in particular, "That's a lie!" To my surprise, Pete and Jane both spoke up. "No," they said in unison, "it's not."

"If it's true," he retorted, "who is my twin?! At least finish off the lie." Earl ranted a while before he calmed enough to let me finish. "Amnon, umm… Your grandfather, he took one of my twins." I stopped, hoping to let it sink in. Earl still seemed confused. "Are you trying to say that he," James pointed at Earl, "is my twin?"

I hung my head ashamed that the secrets I'd carried so many years had broken my children in a matter of seconds. "Grandfather was right, you ARE an ape! I guess you plan to drag my family through the mud with you. Well let me tell you one thing, just because you wallow in filth, that's not an excuse to try and pull us in!" Suzie's words hurt me, but I deserved it all. I'd earned their rebuke and if I hoped to be redeemed, I'd have to accept it and pray that somehow forgiveness would be gifted to me before I took my last breath.

*\* \* \**

*I became my father*
*Now I have knowledge of myself*
*\* \* \**

# CHAPTER 33

I'll be the first to admit that Earl and James being twins sounds suspect. I went home confused beyond belief, but strangely I knew Tamar was telling us the truth. Raw, unfiltered, unbridled truth. My grandfather was a sick man. I knew how much he hated them. And the darker they were, the more he hated them. Tamar was the darkest thing I'd ever seen and I hated her for it. I hated her because for the first time I heard my mother say she was my mother. I hated her because I saw every dimple, mole, curl, and angle in her face. I hated her because I'd long seen myself as colorless... without blemish. Yet here I was staring into a chocolate dipped mirror, and she stared back at me.

I know everything about how love conquers hate, but who was I able to love at that point? I had loved my father who I now knew to be too cowardly to protect the woman he loved. Or maybe he had believed that he was protecting her. Maybe he did what so many people did back then, and do now... Go along to get along. Whatever the case, I now understood what I never believed needed to be understood. I understood the internal struggle that so many Black people in the U.S. felt.

Seeing the real me now meant hating myself only because I had been taught to hate it.

The full lips that had once been colored scarlet and admired by many had not changed, but somehow reminded me of the grossly exaggerated lips of minstrels I'd seen on advertisements as a child. The curves of my body suddenly resembled the brown ones covered in sack cloth and dirt on the pages of national geographic. They had always been subhuman… animal like… unworthy of respect. But now I was one of them. Fully human, loved and created by the divine; yet rejected as the image of God. Reality sank in and my mind swirled. I was Black. I could drink it off, or sleep it off, but when I opened my eyes tomorrow I would still be Black.

There was an ocean of identity lying somewhere between who I knew I was and who I'd believed that I was. While it might take a lifetime for me to cross that ocean I knew that it had to be done. Somehow I had to bridge the gap between the aspects of myself I secretly knew existed but had been programmed to hate, and that which I could no longer deny. There was only one way I believed that I could begin to make my way to the other shore. My journey needed to be a physical one. I had not known my real mother all of these years, but our history had begun across the water. The motherland was calling my name. I needed to make this journey meaningful however. I needed each step to be purposeful, and to reveal to me who I was. I needed this journey to allow me space to forgive myself; to forgive my father; and to forgive God.

I cried. I seethed. I sat in the dark and cried again until there was nothing left to release.

As soon as I was able to catch my breath, I placed an order online that I was certain would change my life forever. I ordered a MatriClan and PatriClan African Ancestry kit. I then called the only man in my family I trusted enough to open up to, and believed would help me find myself.

Pete Jr. answered on the second ring and excitedly allowed me to swab him for the PatriClan test. I needed his Y chromosome to find out what our fathers African ancestry might be, because let's face it, his blood was line was not as pure as he thought it was. I swabbed myself for the MatriClan test and prayed to the God I had yet to forgive that something fruitful might come of this test.

Together Pete and I sent the package in for testing and when I told him goodbye and returned home I closed myself off from the world so that I could be ready when the news of my heritage knocked my socks off. Of course turning my back on the world that I had stupidly become a part of would not be as easy as I had expected. I was unaware of how quickly I would come to understand why my father had stuck it out with the KKK for as long as he had. I would not make the same mistake, but of course there were plenty of mistakes to be made.

*  *  *

*I became my father*
*And for the first time*
*My fear and gratitude go to God*
*And no one else*

*  *  *

# CHAPTER 34

**"I**'m convinced, the best in life is easy." I had chewed on these words all week long, but my mind kept me from accepting the rest. I breathed deeply thanking God for the breath of life, silently pleading that he use me for his work. I began again hoping for some encouragement from the congregants, but their silence pierced my being. Certainly the skeleton I'd recently placed in my closet had not been revealed. "I'm convinced," I searched their faces for the gusto I needed to go on. A few mouths smiled at me, prodding me to go on. I received the warmth of corners of mouths turned up, and tried to hold the gaze of the eyes hovering above them... But the potential for engulfing sadness behind their pupils was shameful. I squeezed my eyes tight hoping to see something different when I opened them. Faces of people who loved me only because they did not know my truth floated aimlessly though the pews. Eyes blinked, noses scrunched and foreheads wrinkled. I blinked again several times, each time squeezing tighter and praying for a different outcome.

Suddenly smiling brown faces transformed into masks stained with the pain of "yes boss" and "naw suh." Smiles always hide humanities greatest sorrows.

Frowned faces disfigured slowly before my very eyes. Nooses hung from ceiling beams, carrying the weight of balls coming in the colors of chocolate, caramel, and toffee with distorted lips; noses struggling for one more breath and eyes bulging with centuries of being America's greatest human resource. Limp bodies adorned with spry spring colors hung lifelessly, waiting to be given the breath of life my family had stolen. Every time I blinked my eyes the picture became more gruesome and I felt sick knowing that I stood breathing but each day my exhalation was suffocating to them. I told myself I saw no color, but I'd lied. I saw color, but only today had I understood what it meant to be so aware of my color that it stole the poetry of the moment.

Had this sight really been what my family enjoyed? Hate was in my history, but it wasn't me. I needed only to convince myself though. The death in the room was grossly unaware that I had transgressed against it. "I'm sorry! I am so sorry!" I cried these words out unconcerned with where they might fall. My heart hoped they reached the heavens, and my soul reached out to every other in the sanctuary. "What have I done?! Forgive me!" Tears streamed like rain in the center of a hurricane… Rhythmically, steadily, and with a vigor that had the potential to destroy everything I touched. "I'm desperate for your forgiveness Lord."

The congregants stared on in astonishment. While everyone knew that the Spirit of God was moving, no one understood what that movement meant for me. Quite frankly I can't say I did either. I heard a voice shouting hallelujah and then thunderous clapping. Drums played and the organ bellowed until I could control my steps no longer and the melodic beat from tambourines commanded my feet to dance to a rhythm God wrote only for me.

A frightening calm washed over me and my soul was electrified… Again, I felt a fire within me. And when I opened my eyes I saw that the sea of brown my family had sought to destroy displayed a sorrowful beauty I never quite perceived until now. Here, people downtrodden in every way had been freed by Jesus the Christ who was just as black as they. This was the clarity people prayed for. And just like the grace I knew God had just shown me, their love was easy. They knew the skin beneath my families sheets yet they still praised God for my deliverance. I was supposed to lead them, but somehow the beauty in their captivated liberty had led me to my own freedom. The easy part was over, dropping my shackles. But difficulty as always was just around the bend. Still I relished the moment, seeing God in the eye of this storm of joy.

God's grace, like their love was easy… It was my own forgiveness that was hard.

I looked to my left, walked over to my brother James and embraced him. I had been serving at the church with him for almost a year now, and I was grateful that my brother had seen fit to lead me back to the God whose grace had been sufficient for me.

*I became my father*
*And I never even knew it*
*I became my father*
*And only Jesus helped me do it*
*His father gave him the gift of brokenness*
*And he blessed me with fragments of my own*
*He handed me the imperfections of humanness*
*And I developed flaws to be shown*
*I swallowed his despair*
*Chewed on his anger*
*And inhaled his confusion*
*I grasped for fresh air*
*Clawed for sanity*
*And lifted my voice in confession*
*I became my father*
*And I didn't want to*
*I became my father*
*And I'm still me too*
*That which I hated*
*I have become*
*That which I feared*
*I came from*
*That which hurt me*
*Has taken me over*
*That which abandoned me*
*Is also my cover*
*I became my father*
*By no fault of my own*
*I became my father*
*And my, how my soul has grown*
*I resisted the mirrors before me*
*Desiring not to know the truth*
*I shielded my eyes from the light*
*Denying the realness of proof*
*I blamed him for what I felt*
*Forgetting that I came forth from his seed*
*I blamed him for fatherly heartbreak*
*But it is brokenness that I need*
*I became my father*
*When I came to know Christ*

*I became my father*
*When I fell to my knees that night*
*I became my father*
*Then yielded to God's reign*
*I became my father*
*When I welcomed my pain*
*I became my father*
*When I knew I wasn't good enough*
*I became my father*
*And I lost the value in stuff*
*Where pain and healing dwell together*
*There my father is I*
*Where confusion and certainty mix*
*Our souls simultaneously cry*
*I strolled through life afraid*
*And finally I swallowed my fear*
*Through the shards of glass that were myself*
*I finally stared deep into the mirror*
*And I saw myself un-whole*
*I saw the joy that had once been there*
*Joy my bitterness stole*
*I saw myself walking, wounded and weak*
*I had no strength or power*
*And here, I thought I was meek*
*Pieces of myself dripping with hurt*
*Floated through a lake of fire blazing sin*
*I looked good on the outside*
*By my mess was within*
*I became my father*
*I was an aware and now free to go*
*I became my faither*
*And I found God in my pieces*
*I became my father*
*And I finally know who* **I** *is*
*I became my father*
*Now I have knowledge of myself*
*I became my father*
*And for the first time*
*My fear and gratitude go to God*
*And no one else*

# Epilogue

I'd walked away from the backward beauty of Shubuta, Mississippi 36 years ago and had found my peace in Denver. Certainly, the day I left Shubuta I thought I'd be leaving Mississippi forever, but no matter how far I went, the solitude of antebellum homes always lured me back. Who would have believed that the floodgates of my past would open washing my shallow faith away, and causing a birth of oceanic liberation? That it would be the driving force to my return home.

My family had its issues, but I'd never met a family that was perfect. My wife and best friend had long since forgiven me, and it had been a year of painful internal searching. Was I to blame for my family's secrets? More importantly, was I capable of the kind of hate… the blatant disregard for the beauty of God's creation that my family had carried?

I couldn't speak for my younger brothers and sisters who were in so deep there was no more "walking away." I prayed they wouldn't carry the same weight my father carried, and nearly lost his life trying to redeem himself from. Only Jesus could save them now, but he had already saved me. Lambs blood, stained my doorpost, and I would be eternally blessed to see that human blood did not stain my hands.

Hallelujah! I was no better than the others, I was merely different. Finally, I took a complete step away from the shackles that had me bound and weighted down. Liberty was intoxicating. For the first time since I returned home, I breathed in the breath of God who'd shared His wind with me.

I drank from His cup, took in His essence and breathed His presence on the world around me.

Redemption was finally real.

www.ingramcontent.com/pod-product-compliance
Lightning Source LLC
Chambersburg PA
CBHW030246030426
42336CB00009B/272